A Journey Through A Life

From Dentistry to Medicine through the dawn of Maxillofacial Surgery to Hospital Management

Russell Hopkins

All Rights Reserved

No part of this book may be reproduced, stored in a retrieval system, or transmitted, in any form or by any means, electronic, mechanical, photocopying, recording or otherwise without prior permission of the author who is the copyright owner.

The Author asserts his moral right to be identified as the author of this work.

ISBN: 978-149-606-3137

Sorejaw Publication

Copyright © Russell Hopkins 2014

In memory of my parents, Charles and Doris Hopkins, and my sister Irene

This memoir is dedicated to my wife Jill and Richard, Claire and Robert

Contents

1. Family and Early Childhood — 1
2. School and World War Two — 8
3. Boarding School — 12
4. University Dental Training — 24
5. First Job in Dental Practice, and Increasing Disillusionment — 31
6. Dental Practice in Rhodesia — 35
7. Nottingham, My First Job in Oral Surgery — 40
8. Dental Fellowship and Oral Surgery Registrar in Chertsey — 44
9. Back to School, Medical Student — 51
10. Part Time Dental Practice and a Brush with the General Dental Council — 55
11. House Physician Croydon, House Surgeon Wandsworth — 58
12. Life as a Ship's Surgeon, Quite a Different World — 65
13. Senior Registrar - A Training Post ? — 74
14. Consultant in Cardiff - A Fresh Start in an Alien Environment — 77
15. Junior Trainees in Cardiff — 92
16. The Early Days of my Involvement in Medical Politics — 95
17. Overseas Lecture Tours - USA, India, South Africa and Hong Kong — 97
18. Saudi Arabia - Local and Long Term Problems — 102
19. President of the British Association of Oral and Maxillofacial Surgeons — 106
20. A Change of Job - General Manager of the University Hospital of Wales — 109

21. The Management Summary   124
22. Chairman of Glan-y-Môr Trust and the
             Battle for Neath General Hospital   129
23. The Impact of the New Labour Government of 1997   140
24. The Bro Morgannwg Trust - A Difficult Start
             but a Strong Finish   142
25. Conclusion   152
26. An Unwelcome Finale   153

Appendix 1   How No One Acted When
        They Should Have   157
Appendix 2   A Memorable Patient in the
        Bad Old Days   161
Appendix 3 A Personal View of Today's NHS   163
Appendix 4 Daily Telegraph Article   170

I acknowledge, with thanks, Sue Jones who converted my handwritten drafts into a legible typescript and Gwyneth who advised me this was a tale worth telling. Andrew Sadler for his stimulus to produce this memoir and his editorial work and Maralyn Sadler for reading the proofs.

Russell Hopkins 2014

1 Family and Early Childhood

September 19th 2007 – it is a rainy cold autumnal day matched by the arthritis of my thumb and first finger holding this pen. I am 75 and the realisation that my life cannot go on forever tempts me to put pen to paper so that my children and their children may understand me a little better as well as having a window into a world that has changed so much during my lifetime. Cherie Blair said, 'It feels wrong, after an eventful life, just to let it pass as if the journey had no meaning.' I agree.

I was born in 45 Ettrick Grove, Sunderland at 8.30am on 30th April, 1932, on the double bed in the back bedroom used by my parents, Charles Albert and Frances Doris Hopkins (née Baldwin). My father, then the General Manager of Sunderland Corporation Transport, had previously held the same post in Wigan. Unusually for the time, he had been divorced when he met my mother, who was a secretary in the Wigan office. Born on February 14th 1886, he was 12 years older than her – a handsome, dominant, dark haired individual, features which may have contributed to his belief that somewhere in his antecedents there was Spanish blood. My father was certainly quick to anger but also quick to cool. He smoked the weak Craven A cigarettes but only with a half pint of beer. He sought the company of his peers each evening and at weekends in the public house or the golf club but it was rare for us to notice anything untoward when he returned home. Moderate drinking and smoking was the order and rarely at home.

My paternal grandparents were already gone by then but once my father took me to the farm in Wiltshire where they had lived and where his father had been the bailiff. It was on top of a hill called Gallows Top, for the obvious reason that nearby was an old site of execution. From the farm my father walked the three miles to and from the school where he learned his three Rs whilst at weekends he helped out on the farm. Father was the last of nine children, the other eight being girls. I cannot remember how many survived but I did meet three of them and their children in Swindon. My father's first job was as a boiler boy with the Swindon Light Railways or tramways. He must have impressed for he moved up through the organisation.

He did not fight in World War I; he was 30 in 1914 and was considered sufficiently important to be granted exemption from army service. This resulted, on at least one occasion, in having a white feather pushed into his hand by an unknown female seeking yet more death and sacrifice. The use of the white feather emblematic of cowardice was used indiscriminately and even given to soldiers wearing civvies on leave.

My Father Charles   **My Mother Doris**

I know nothing of my father's first marriage other than that my mother always hated the realisation that my father had 'known' another woman. My father joined Wigan Corporation Transport as Chief Clerk and then became General Manager after which he married my mother who worked in the office. My sister, Irene Gwendoline, was born on November 27th 1929, I believe in Wigan.

My mother, Frances Doris, was the daughter of John Baldwin of 74 Widdrington Road, Monument Park, Wigan. Her mother had died from cancer at an early age but not before she taught her daughter that sex and periods were crosses women had to bear. Before having children my mother suffered from unpleasant dysmenorrhoea and she endured sex along with many Victorian women; she regarded it as an unpleasant wifely duty which cannot have satisfied my father. Her brother, Uncle Charlie, had a history of recurrent chest problems of which he died in late middle age. I met him a few times when he came to stay – a pleasant unassuming individual. I don't believe he was married.

My maternal grandfather, John Baldwin, was a clerk with the Great Western Railway. He lived alone after Charlie died and came once a year to stay in Sunderland. My memory is of an old man, small in stature, with a thick moustache and smoking a pipe. He would sit in the leather armchair next to the radio in the dining room where there was a coal fire in the winter, puffing away on a pipe filled with Erinmore tobacco. This came in compressed sheets and rubbing these in the palm of my hands not only assisted my grandfather but released a rich aroma of tobacco leaf and malt which I enjoyed. John lived to be 74. I don't know what killed him. He owned his house and my mother received the small sum raised from its sale. My recollection of him being an old man makes me wonder what do my grandchildren think of me – do I look that old?

Despite having a working class background, my grandmother bred in my mother the need for standards of speech and good manners, both in behaviour and at the table, backed up with an unquestioning belief in God and the 10 commandments. My mother believed in high Anglicanism, creationism, the requirement of helping one's fellowmen and women, of churchgoing and the purity of all women and a few men in the Church of God – Catholic or Protestant. My father was not so naive but even he said his prayers before sleep. Both were excellent writers, good spellers and capable, if basic, mathematicians. My father read the Daily Mail and the News of the World which my mother detested on principle.

I was conceived and born on the same sprung horsehair mattress upon which thirty eight years later my wife conceived our first born. My parents used a feather mattress on top of the main mattress. I suspect this was removed for my birth which happened quickly with only the midwife present. The GP, Dr. Nichol, arrived after the event. My mother was proud of her expertise and of maintaining her privacy and dignity. I was breast-fed and a tranquil baby, or I was until about one year old when I developed whooping cough of such malevolence that Dr. Nichol told my mother later that he had not expected my survival. Mother believed I had caught the disease because the bedroom window was left open with a cold north easterly blowing. She did not know about viruses and bugs. My illness was nursed at home by mother and my survival must have depended upon the legacy of her breast milk and her loving care, for there were no suitable medicines or a children's hospital with a respiratory unit. Whooping cough carried a significant mortality rate – I was lucky.

My early childhood memories are few and vague. Semi-reliable memories come from when I was about four onwards. Every winter I had some form of chest infection which continued to my early teens. My mother would rub my chest with eucalyptus oil for me to inhale the vapour. The coldness of houses in the winter without central heating or adequate insulation must have been a factor. The winters were cold with long periods of inclement freezing weather.

Beneath Sunderland, and much of Durham County, lay the coalfield; a few miles away from us was Silksworth Pit. With the right wind its hooter could be heard announcing the end of the shift. Well within an hour men in their work clothes, black with coal dust, walked past our house on their way home. Miners could always get a seat on a tram for nobody wanted to sit beside or squeeze by them. Pithead baths and working clothes lay in the future, as did the coal allowance. A common sight was a male pushing a bicycle or pram carrying a sack containing coal scavenged from tips of coal waste. Pits on the coast discharged their waste into the sea; the rocks sank but pieces of coal and much coal dust was washed to the beach where locals harvested it.

My mother ordered deliveries of coal, one ton at a time. It was transported in one hundredweight bags, each one slung over the shoulder of the coalman, who was as black as a miner, and dumped into our coal house. Mother took care to count in each bag for it was common practice to under-deliver the order for home use or for sale. Some merchants delivered coal with significant amounts of rock included; Mother would not use them again. I remember the weights and measures people coming to weigh the coal to confirm short delivery; a prosecution would follow.

Nobody was really warm in the winter; house insulation lay well into the future. It was alleged that some working class males covered themselves in pig grease and put on woollen vests and pants which stayed on until the spring. Conversely I remember seeing, in the summer, young male children without trousers in public and children of both sexes without shoes. Poverty was poverty then, quite unlike the so called poverty of today. Drunkenness was common and most adult males smoked the cheapest Woodbines, sold in packets of five, adding to the list of the causes of early death.

Ettrick Grove, built on a down slope, was a single line of semi-detached houses separating a council estate from both Barnes Park and the playing fields of Bede Grammar School. The other half of our building was domiciled by its builder, Mr. Elliott, and his family. For reasons unknown and not understood by me, my father was averse to owning his house or having life insurance. Our house, therefore, was rented which became a major difficulty after my father's early death. I believe my father always thought he would leave Sunderland and move on. However, he declined to take a similar post in Blackpool when it was offered.

Directly in front of our houses was an enclosed patch of land filled with evergreen bushes in which we played and to our left there were half a dozen larger buildings each containing two shops with flats from which my mother obtained her supplies. Butcher, baker, confectioners, hardware, grocer, fruiterers and post office, off licence, chemist, newsagent and fish and chip shop. Cod and chips cost one penny and plaice and chips three pennies. My mother said the workers eat cod! The nearby bakers made and baked their bread and confectionery in the converted garage so that at the bottom of our long garden the smell of baking was mouthwatering. Street lighting was by gas and the gas lighter came with his long pole twice a day to turn the lamps on or off. Several of our supplies came in horse-drawn cabs or wagons. The milk came in carts, in large milk cans from which milk was dispensed into jugs which were covered with a crocheted lead-weighted cotton cover. Pasteurised, bottled milk was a later development. My sister developed bovine tuberculosis in the lymph glands of her neck from milk. Her surgeon made a long vertical incision which left an ugly scar. Ringtons Tea had a very smart cab and horse, whilst the horses pulling the coal cart were big and strong. My mother prized horse manure for her roses and would go out with a shovel and bucket. The rag and bone man was a regular street caller driving a rickety cart pulled by a despairing horse. Supplies to the off licence arrived on a large cart pulled by two huge greys.

Our house had four bedrooms. Initially I slept in a cot and later a single bed in the front bedroom in which there was a double bed for guests, which much later became mine. Initially, I believe my sister had slept in it but she moved into the smaller front bedroom as she became a young lady. The fourth back bedroom was the box room and storeroom.

Before the war we had a series of live-in maids, young girls from working class homes whose mothers answered my mother's advertisement. Mother taught them to lay the table, bring in the food and take away and wash the dishes. They did the house cleaning and bed making along with Mother. She also taught them the basics of cooking at which she was good. When we had guests to stay I had to sleep with the maid in the double bed in the front bedroom. My sister must have slept with my parents. My sleep was extremely innocent although one girl did catch me watching her get undressed. Maids left for a variety of reasons, mainly for better jobs but occasionally because of dishonesty or the bloody mindedness of teenagers. For many young girls domestic service was their first job after leaving school.

Breakfast and weekday meals were eaten in the kitchen in front of the coal fire which heated the water boiler which also warmed the bathroom tank and w.c. upstairs. The built-in oven's door was assiduously black-leaded by the maid or char-lady. Cooking was normally done on the gas stove but turkeys or bread were cooked in the oven.

At weekends meals were taken in the dining room in which there would be a coal fire in the winter. The dining room had a large alcove with glass French windows and could be closed off by thick velvet curtains. My sister and I would use the alcove to put on shows for my parents and friends using the curtains as stage curtains. In the dining room was the wireless powered by acid filled batteries that had to be taken away to be charged. A large wired aerial extended down the whole of the garden and I would play with the knobs to pick up new stations. At Christmas we would gather to listen to the King's speech as we did in September 1939 when Chamberlain told us that a state of war now existed between the UK and Germany. I was seven and remember this broadcast and asking my father what 'war' meant. It was not long before I found out.

The first manifestation of war was the air raid siren which sounded soon after Chamberlain ceased broadcasting. Apparently nationwide I had no knowledge of what was intended. The second manifestation was the blackout, my mother put up drapes to go with the curtains, later we had various fitted boards to put inside the windows. The third manifestation was the three crucifixes put up over our beds to keep us safe at night; mine remains in my study on the mantelpiece, a memento of my childhood, the war, my mother and my survival for 82 years against the odds.

In those happy days we were allowed to go out to play. My sister's group of friends were older than mine. My pals were mainly from the adjacent council estate from whom I learned the tricks of the trade. I became aware in several ways that I was privileged when compared with some of my play-mates from across the road. At Christmas I realised that they put up their stockings for presents whilst my sister and I left pillow cases on the end of our beds. I always had had one 'big' present from my parents, e.g. a fort with solders, a clockwork train or Meccano set, with which one could fabricate many objects. Small gifts from my sister, friends and relations, e.g. sweets or chocolates or picture books, were also welcomed. I believe these few presents meant more to us than the masses of presents required to please parents and children today. The significance of Christmas has all but gone under the pressure of spending.

I am ashamed to remember that when my sister was given a doll I kept up a snivelling campaign until I too got one. Of course when I got it I had no love for it at all and even then I knew I had been a fool. I also remember deciding that I would give up snivelling and crying about nothing. I wonder if my parents noticed any difference.

At the top of the grove there was a blue police kiosk from which the beat officer reported to the station. When he was wanted, a blue light would flash from its top. Policemen then walked or cycled around the patch and were familiar figures – part of the landscape. Our policeman for a long time was Sparky, an ex-serviceman with medal ribbons and a pointed, waxed moustache. When Sparky caught a child committing a misdemeanour, he would give chase and strike the miscreant with his cape which he carried over his shoulder. This usually knocked you over. I never received any sympathy from my father who would add a couple of blows of his own if we had done something like breaking a window.

My mother was Anglican. We were trotted out every Sunday in our best clothes to Matins in the morning and Sunday school in the afternoon. My newest shoes were worn only for church and then came into general use when the old pair were worn out or too small. This resulted in my wearing shoes which were usually too small. They would be stretched but probably highly unsuitable, contributing in later life to my ugly hallux valgus deformity of both feet.

Music featured in the house with a stand-up piano in the drawing room which we still have. Mother was a moderate pianist but an excellent amateur soprano and musical evenings with friends were common. They would gather in the drawing room and sing or play their instruments. My sister and I were required to sit and listen, much to our horror. Our only relief was Mr. Snowdon, a violinist, who made loud nasal sounds as he breathed in and out causing us to ache with the effort of not laughing. My father was never present. My mother would frequently sing solo anthems at church and every Easter 'I know that my redeemer liveth' by Handel would cause me severe apprehension until she had achieved her top G♯. Mother sang with the Sunderland Choral Society and I could have been a star for I was recruited to play Elijah's dead son. Alas I would not keep still and was replaced by my sister in her first starring role.

2 School and World War Two

Sometime about four or five, I was enrolled in the Montessori School at St. Anthony's, run by a female Catholic order. I remember the delight I had sitting on the floor when I tied my first bow on a frame of ribbons. I did not last long, however, for on Armistice Day at 11 o'clock I went up to Mother Superior who was praying aloud and told her my Daddy said nobody was to make any noise for two minutes until the gun went again. She was not amused by this Anglican impertinence.

My next school was Argyle House, a private establishment for boys 6-12 years of age in a large multi-storey house in St. George's Square. There I met Jimmy Taylor, the surviving son of a successful businessman in Sunderland and owner of laundries. Automatic washers did not exist then and for those who could afford it, household washing and dry cleaning was collected and delivered by van. My mother and maid or charlady did our wash every Monday morning. Clothes were initially soaked in warm soapy water in large zinc tubs and agitated by a long handled wooden implement with five legs sticking out from the bottom. This implement was rotated by hand to loosen the dirt; whites were then boiled. Neck collars and dirty bits were scrubbed. It was hard work.. The wringer was hand turned to squeeze out the water Afterwards the clothes were hung out to dry and later aired on a rack in the kitchen after ironing. I remember the arrival of our first electric washing machine which had a motorised wringer. The char would frequently feed her fingers into it and be trapped by the wrist. My mother would bind her wrist in a bandage soaked in vinegar and saltpetre. All sprains were similarly treated, though I am sure the liquid was of no benefit.

Jimmy Taylor and I became firm friends and we encouraged each other in idleness. He lived out of town at South Hylton and I would take two buses, costing ½ d and 1d to get there. He had a loft playroom full of toys and plenty of room in the spacious grounds to get up to mischief which we did for many years.

Argyle House was also known as Hannah's, after the two sisters who owned it. The school colours on the compulsory uniform and caps were green and yellow which stood out amongst the children going to and from other schools. I went there by tram and usually late because of my life long inability to go to bed early and get up with plenty of time to get ready. My usual excuse was to blame the tram which was late, full, had either come off the line or lost its cable. Even the teachers drew my attention to my father being in charge. I remember little about this time at school other than that my term reports always suggested I could do better, and the large crater left by the bomb which totally destroyed it and killed the caretaker in 1941. I was much disturbed by the reopening of the school in another large house about a mile away only 10 days later.

After the occupation of Northern Europe by the Germans, the Scottish and north east ports and ship building areas were repeatedly attacked at night by German bombers. As our house overlooked Sunderland these air raids were marvellous firework displays with searchlights, tracer shells from the Bolfors light ack ack, parachute flares and the flashes of the heavy ack ack shells. There was a battery of heavies sited on the nearby farm which supplied our milk. The crack of these guns firing was awe inspiring. My sister and I slept in our concrete slab shelter at the bottom of the garden which was always damp and full of mosquitoes. My parents would come down from the house when the siren sounded and my father had a lucky escape when on his own he fell down the steps and landed with his head in the sump which was full of water.

Static air defences included large balloons which occasionally would break free on a windy day and be shot down in flames by fighters from Usworth Aerodrome and a smoke screen produced by burning crude oil on the windward side of town. The dirty smoke on a cold moonlit winter night was unpleasant as well as useless and we were delighted when it was stopped.

Shrapnel came down all over the place. After a raid we boys would search for it. We affected to know which came from a bomb or a shell. Bomb splinters being rare were much more valuable in the trading that followed. I remember walking through Fawcett Street the morning after a heavy raid in which several large stores had burnt out. The rank smell of fire was everywhere. Beside the railway station was a goods wagon blown through the open roof. I was mightily impressed.

As the war continued Father bought a Morrison table shelter which took over our dining table. This had thick angled steel legs bolted to a steel base and top. The sides were steel mesh which could be lifted off to allow access and eating off the top. This shelter had the advantage of being warm and dry with easy access when the sirens sounded. My parents found me asleep on the stairs more than once as a result. Often we heard the bombers before the sirens went.

I remember one particularly noisy raid with fearsome explosions quite nearby which shook the house. I realised my father was shaking quite violently and I asked him why? It was my mother who explained that Daddy was worrying about Irene and me. My understanding of death and its consequences were limited and the reality was that if you were a child and not hit these raids were exciting! There was a lot of gossip and grumbling that our fighter protection had been sent south leaving us without cover. The reality was that night fighters were not plentiful or successful. Bombing raids usually accompanied moonlight and decent weather and a good night's sleep was usually possible when conditions were otherwise. Intruder flights caused disturbance but little bombing. My mother used to invite the Poles and Czechoslovakians from the squadrons at Usworth aerodrome, now the home of Nissan, to afternoon tea. I was in awe of them and their fighter planes.

Before the war our summer holidays were usually spent on a farm on the south coast of England. We would drive there in father's Austin 6 and when I was sleepy I would lie on the carpet in the passenger foot well and sleep soundly warmed by the engine. I loved to return the salute of the AA man and would stand and give a full military response. During the war our holidays were spent on farms in the country about 40/50 miles away. I loved these times: the horses, the harvest, helping with milking. I don't know if I inherited this from my paternal grandfather but I do know that the country life has always attracted me. We were on a southern farm in 1939 when rumours of war became strong and we returned to Sunderland prematurely, my father driving home without an overnight rest. It is worth remembering that the A1 was a difficult and dangerous road then.

Both my parents believed in God and my mother certainly practised her Christianity. She constantly helped people and charities and would often pass a hot meal to Mrs. Fraser, the widow of a dentist who had died of typhoid in Gallipoli, and who lived next door. It was either during the war or just after that when mother asked me to climb over our intervening six foot fence one windy winter night to see if I could see Mrs. Fraser who had not answered her doorbell. Through the back window I could see her lying on the floor with her head in the fireplace. I came back over the fence as if it were two foot high. Mrs. Fraser had been dead for some time, having had a stroke as she lit the fire. I had disturbed nights for some time after.

My parents were typical of their age, believing that children had to be guided and brought up rather than leaving them to do their own thing. My mother believed in my telling the truth and, for example, when I denied eating a newly baked scone without permission, I had to stay in the pantry looking for it until I owned up. She was not averse to giving me a slap on the legs if I drove her too far but she left the physical punishment to my father which was probably unfair on him. He was quick to anger and when he lost it I was extremely frightened. Formal punishments followed my worst misdemeanours or bad school reports and involved my having my bare backside struck with my braces one or two times. Two of my crimes I remember. I used an old bus and tram pass of my father's to get free travel, keeping the money given to me. Like an idiot I used the pass with a conductor who knew me – never again. My second, and infinitely more serious, was a short period of shoplifting Dinky toys from Saxons. In this crime I led Adam Gray, another friend. When our parents noticed an unexplained increase in these relatively expensive toy models, retribution soon followed. The lesson was well learned and I never repeated the practice. Despite these beatings, I never ceased to love my father and mother and I have much to thank them for. I still look at their photographs with gratitude and pleasure. We had 'rough and tumble' on a Sunday afternoon after father had his post-prandial kip. I loved going to work with him and on his tours of bus and tram depots. He taught me to drive a motor car before I was twelve. His instructions started as soon as I was big enough to lean over to steer the car or to change the gears by moving the stick whilst he did the clutch and this in the days of double declutching. Later when my parents came to see me at boarding school and to take me out for a picnic, he let me drive the car on the moorlands roads. His instruction got me through my driving test first time on my 17th birthday – alas he was dead by then. I realised long ago how much I owed my parents and the influence they had on the way I lived my life and practised my profession. This did not make me a saint. They were patriots and proud of the British Empire. They stood up when the National Anthem played on the radio. We will not see their like again.

3. Boarding School

As the war proceeded so did my education, albeit badly. Jimmy was bottom of the form and I second bottom. My promise as reported by teachers remained a promise. My father decided that I should go away to school when I was twelve. Mr. Birkbeck MA Cantab, known as Kip, Headmaster of Barnard Castle School, accepted me for the summer term of 1944. I found myself in a school with about 350 boarders and 50-60 day boys close to the River Tees in lovely country but in the middle of a huge army camp. This was a training area for our new army. Infantry and mechanised units were in camps all around and frequent raids by the police and headmaster upon our lockers would produce a bewildering mix of ammunition, gun sights and other war paraphernalia nicked from the tanks and armoured cars. No one was expelled, just beaten – it was a hazard of war. The army was everywhere and suddenly the convoys disappeared from the roads and all became quiet; then we heard of 'D' day and the invasion.

I settled into school life and its austerity without homesickness, though I usually managed a sob or two when my parents left me after a visit. I had been placed in Northumberland House which surprised me as I came from Durham, the other three houses being Durham, York and Teesdale for the day boys. I slept in 'J' dorm, the junior open dormitory with its monitor and sub-monitor. The two sets of washbasins in the middle supplied only cold water. There were two wall mounted urinals at one end and for no.2s you had to leave the dormitory and go to the nearest 'bog'. The porters were 'boglers' and the maids 'skivvies'. There were two mandatory showers a week and one hot bath but if one indulged in sport, showers were more frequent. We had a change of underclothes and shirt once a week, unless anything untoward occurred. It was all a bit primitive looking back but character building. The boglers cleaned our shoes. There were no fags. Very quickly male nudity became normal to me in the swimming baths and showers. I was always hungry and my mother's supplies for my tuck box essential for life. School meals were pretty awful, food devalued by mass cooking and prolonged heating. Masters sat at the head of each table at lunch whilst the monitors and sub-monitors took over at other meals. The Head gave the Grace in Latin at the beginning and end of the meal. The huge dining room walls were covered with the names of school 1st teams to which my own name would be added five years later.

The school, classed as a minor public, was founded in 1884; it had established traditions and practices of public schools which I absorbed easily. Dress was grey shorts or trousers plus jackets but on Sundays pinstripe trousers and black jackets. The school colours were blue and brown. The masters were too old or unfit for military service, mostly nearing the end of their careers or brought back out of retirement. 'Bish' Adlard, our Housemaster, was one such; his nickname coming from the noise escaping from him when he laughed. Housemasters doled out our pocket money each Wednesday and Saturday, keeping a record in a little book. They gave guidance and discipline to their brood. They were empowered to beat us. Masters and monitors entered our names in the house book for misdemeanours and three entries in short term required a visit to the Housemaster. Bish gave me three on my pyjama covered backside with a sand shoe which stung considerably. It worked for I was not beaten again. The monitors, however, carried on the practice quite unofficially and without such restraint.

That first term for me was a major change in life. I had no Jimmy to waste time with. I played cricket and took part in other sporting activities and walked up and down the tree covered river banks. What I did not do was to become an academic. The term soon reached half way when we had a week at home using the steam train each way. I had no tears for my return for I was enjoying life. As we neared the term end I became increasingly apprehensive about the ritual new kids had to endure on the last night. About a week before term end and after we had assembled in the Chapel, the Head announced the death of a boy from 'J' dorm and the acute illness of another, both with meningitis. The school was to break up immediately. Again I was lucky to have avoided death and the last night of term.

After a summer holiday of playing with Jimmy who had been sent to school in Sheringham in Norfolk, I returned for the autumn term. To please my mother I had joined the chapel choir as a treble and was confirmed by the Bishop of Durham into the Church of England. I also joined the Junior Training Crops. My 1918 Lee Enfield rifle was heavy. I started to play rugby and for a short time was a forward. However, a scrum collapsed and my head bent under me until I thought it would come off. I was scared even though I knew nothing about broken necks. I never played in the forwards again. The school excelled at rugby even then and I never got beyond the 2nd XV.

The school chapel had been built by the old boys to commemorate those killed in World War 1. It became quite common as 1944 moved into 1945 for the Head to announce yet another death of an old boy and call for a minute of silence. Empty wall panels awaited a fresh crop of names. It seemed the war would never end and I did not want it to for I wanted to be a Spitfire pilot. Death had no meaning to me.

Being in the choir meant we led the hymns of the morning and evening assemblies in chapel. On Sunday, Matins at 10.45am and Evensong at 3.45pm involved more singing. The content of the service never involved me intellectually or spiritually but I always watched the padre as he gave the evening blessing, which to this day still brings a lump to my throat when I hear it on the radio.

Chapel was not without its lighter moments. Then the organ was hand pumped by boys who got out of being in the Service. They tended to have more initiative than academic ability. They were not so clever, however, for as they pumped so did they smoke and out from the pipes of the organ came a cloud of cigarette smoke enveloping Mr. Heywood, the bursar and organist, and reaching the Headmaster. There were physical consequences for them but laughter for us. There remained a few smokers who puffed away in the bogs and the cycle shed behind the pavilion but strangely I gave up smoking my father's cigarettes when I went away to school and did not start again until I was 23 years old.

I do not remember when it started but to my surprise I found myself rising up my form after term exams. It was not that I became a swot; it was just that sometimes there was nothing better to do. Anything that avoided mathematics or hard work seemed to suit me. I came top in Scripture which made my mother wonder if I would go into the Church.

To my extreme embarrassment, in my young life, I had occasionally wet my bed at night and this occurred now and again during my first term. Thank goodness my second term was not complicated by the same problem which had disappeared for good. I often wondered what the basis for this was and if my father's temper had anything to do with it. I suspect physiology rather than psychology. What remained was a tendency for me to develop chest infections towards Christmas time and I did this at school. I don't believe my lungs were aided by having to have the dormitory windows open even in the winter and waking up with snow on the bed and ice on the inside of the window.

Early in my school career, perhaps when I was 13, I became sick towards the end of the Christmas term. I knew I was ill and should go to the San but I wanted to get home so I stuck it out. I could not swallow food because of pain and breathing was difficult. I was wretched. The night before school broke up I had a terrible nightmare and the monitor found me lying with my head between the vertical bars of the metal bed head. The next day I got home by train assisted by friends and went straight to bed. The GP, Dr. Dalgleash, found I had a consolidated lobe of my right lung. I had had lobar pneumonia which untreated had gone through its natural course including a crisis which produced my nightmare. I remember the shock I had when I heard the diagnosis. Gradually I recovered and residual bronchiectasis cleared after several weeks. I returned to school at the end of the holidays, now with glasses to correct astigmatism and long sightedness.

Adam Gray, a pal from Argyle House School, had joined the school and Northumberland House. He was homesick at first, crying every night. I must have had the germ of a caring nature for I used to comfort him. There were always a few new kids who cried every night until they settled. Did this separation from their mothers do them harm? Adam sent his own sons to Barney, so he must not have believed he suffered – or perhaps he forgot? After being away at school I was never upset at having to leave home nor did I feel tied to my home area. There were lads called up for National Service who wept for their mothers at night whereas the public school boys took to Service life and the conditions that were probably better than they had endured at school. Barney made me self-sufficient and the discipline it imposed, the wide education it gave me and the sports I played were a real benefit to me. What it did not do, alas, was to rid me of an inherent laziness or give me the realisation that graft was a necessary adjunct to my life.

In my third year I turned up for the Colts cricket nets and caught the eye of the master in charge who liked my bowling action. I hadn't a clue what I was doing but I somehow developed two paces then a skip and then six more paces before I bowled a medium pace natural off break and swing ball. We used a small ball and somehow it worked for me. I was picked for the Colts XI and was disappointed if I didn't get four or more wickets each innings. I loved hearing a departing batsman saying to his replacement, 'The ball is going all over the place.' When I was too old for the Colts the full sized ball did not flatter me. However, I worked hard and became a reasonable fielder and thrower and was a slogger down the order. I made the 1st XI and got my colours which pleased me enormously. I never got beyond the 2nd XV at rugby, playing stand off or full back. I was a kicker without a rugby brain. In one match I determined to fix my opposite number and at the earliest opportunity threw myself at him. Alas, I hit his knee with my head and was poleaxed with a terrible headache. I was taken off shortly afterwards because I was tackling my own people – I could not remember who or where I was or where my glasses were. Worse still, that night was the school play in which I had a part and I stood on stage not knowing what I was doing there, aware only of my headache. Gradually I returned to normality after a couple of days and often wondered just how much brain tissue was lost.

I stayed in the choir and was either first or second in the inter-house Coombs Cup as a treble, alto and finally a tenor. Church music remains a lifelong pleasure even though any religious belief has long gone. The King's College Service of Nine Lessons on Christmas Eve is a must to listen to. My Service in the JCC continued even though 1945 brought the end of World War 2. The world remained dangerous. I soon had stripes and passed the Cert A and a few technical certificates. I got my 1st Class shot crossed-rifles and won both the Churchill Trophy and the Basil Place Cup with .303 on the nearby army range. I was the senior cadet CSM for the last couple of years and looked forward to my National Service. One of my duties as CSM was to collect all failed 'thunder flashes' from training exercises. I took a few of these home and found there was much less powder in the chamber than I expected. I filled one chamber full and stuck the fuses together to gain a reasonable length I then went down to the bottom of the garden where our air raid shelter had been beside the garage and behind the greenhouse. I dug a small hole into the clay and put in the loaded thunder flash, lit the fuse and retired behind the garage. There was an impressive bang followed by a crash as the windows of the greenhouse collapsed. I then knew why they did not put much powder into the chamber in the first place. The one thing that was beyond me was cross country running. Then we wore plimsolls – their rubber soles quite useless on roads. I had flat feet by then, both longitudinal and transverse – and running on a hard surface caused severe pains in my shins which slowed me up resulting in calls to 'get a move on 'you lazy bastard'. These flat feet contributed at a later date to my medical rejection for the National Service even though I played squash, rugby and cricket. A strange world!

However, school is not all about sport and as my aptitude in the non-science subjects developed my skills at mathematics, chemistry and physics were subliminal. The exception was biology and that may have been entirely due to Bentley Beetham. He was a bachelor, small in stature but tough as old boots. He was a sadist who kept control by the use of the knuckle of his middle finger which he would rap upon the skull of any miscreant. He was a self-trained naturalist and mountaineer who had got as far as the base camp of the 1924 Mallory-Irving Everest Expedition until mountain sickness stopped him. He would take the whole form on walks along the Tees, up onto the moors and those who wished to, to Borrowdale to rock climb. I never got into risking my life unnecessarily. On the walks he would point out, show or demonstrate. It was wonderful biology, botany and zoology in the field. His lessons were memorable and I seriously doubt if anybody was not inspired by him even if they were scared stiff. He had a collection of plate photographs he had taken on Everest and would show these to the whole school in the library. This collection still exists and did Mallory reach the top?

Beetham played all the good squash players at which the school excelled. I played him a few times but never got near beating him. He stood in the middle obstructing all the time playing clever little drop shots. No one dared call 'let'. He was a bastard but is remembered by every pupil of his time.

I was delighted when my parents came to watch me playing cricket against Durham School or the Royal Grammar School, Newcastle. It gave me considerable satisfaction to have them present, particularly when I took a wicket or a catch.

I cannot remember how old I was when I first noticed that when my father had a pee he would lean over the pan and wait some time for the urine stream to start. It could take as long for him to fully stop which could be irritating if you wanted to pee yourself. It became the norm for him and I learned he was to go into hospital in Newcastle to put it right. When he returned it did not seem much better and even I noticed his increasing fatigue and bent shoulders when he had a meal after coming in from work. Because I was away at school I was not around to see his walking degenerate but he developed severe backache and in due course leg weakness. He had to stop work and by my 16th birthday he started to sleep downstairs. As we only had an upstairs bathroom this must have been a nursing problem. The significance of all this escaped me for I was not informed what was going on and my ignorance was total. His illness coincided with the Schools Certificate examination for the completion of my secondary schooling. I did not do much work for the exam and was delighted with my six credits, two passes and one fail. I was surprised I had not got a distinction in biology but much more surprised at my credit in maths which I was sure was a mistake!

However, I had matriculated and tore into the room to tell my bedridden father I had passed. By now his legs had failed him yet it did not occur to me he would not get better. When the holidays were over I went back to the 6th form. At some stage during the next term my father was admitted to hospital as he was doubly incontinent and I remember going to visit him at half term. I returned to school and one night I was called to see my housemaster, Stan Hardisty. I was to return home first thing in the morning – my father was ill. The penny dropped at last. By the time I got home my mother told me that he had died that night. I had not had the opportunity to say goodbye or thank you. Something which makes me weep even as I write this.

It is almost impossible for me to explain today how ignorant we were then about medicine in general and cancer in particular. The word was never used until death occurred and patients were not informed. I cannot understand how I did not realise what was going on. My mother who knew did not tell my sister or me, nor did my father know, so that he could not say goodbye either. I never totally forgave my mother even if what she did was normal practice at that time. When my father first noticed difficulty in peeing was the time he should have sought medical advice. By the time he did, he had prostatic secondary deposits in his skeleton and his operation was a palliative orchidectomy and his pills oestrogen. The loss of his testes caused him considerable psychological distress and he was not told why. His incontinence and paralysis of his legs was the result of collapse of his spine because of cancerous deposits. My mother's silence was correct in one way – I don't remember him stripped of all fat and cachexic prior to death but I don't believe that compensated for our not being able to make peace with each other. My mother's death when aged 80 was sudden and due to a ruptured aneurysm so that saying goodbye was impossible. What made that worse was I did not get to her funeral but that is another story. My father's funeral was terrible, sad and too late for me to say farewell.

My father was a man of his time. He had never owned his house or taken out life insurance. Dying at 62 he left my mother without a house, a pension or any obvious means of support. She received my father's superannuation payments and that was it. I did not know then but the Masons paid for my final years of schooling. My mother was ill-prepared to be a widow at the age of 50 and she had a tough time without much assistance from me.

I presume my mother was peri-menopausal and in retrospect she was clinically depressed. 'Oh dear me' was a repeated sign of this but I was too immature to know about depression or grief. Shortly after my father's death my mother told me that on his deathbed he had told her about a relationship he had had with another woman. This played on my mother's psyche and added to her woes even though my father had told her that he believed her to have been a wonderful wife. I expect Father was sexually frustrated for my mother was enamoured of the Virgin Mary. In a fit of anger she bemoaned her situation, cried out she should not have married father – that she had sacrificed her career as a singer for him. Inadvisably I replied she had made her choice and anyway at 30 she would have already been a singer if she had been that good. I certainly regretted my father's deathbed confession. I went to see my father's deputy – who I called Uncle Harry and asked him if he knew anything about this other woman but he denied all knowledge.

It is strange to think of the sexual repression that then existed in a pseudo religious post-Victorian atmosphere. The middle and working class suffered whilst the upper class made whoopee. It is no surprise to know of the thousands of prostitutes that existed at that time and after many women were left without potential husbands by two World Wars. My mother and father on one visit to London were walking down the Strand together when a street lady put her arm through my father's and propositioned him. For years my mother believed this meant that my father knew her despite my worldly protestations to the contrary. She gave me only one lesson on sex and that was when I was 29! All she said was that she hoped that I always behaved as a gentleman.

A legacy of my mother's disquiet and her financial difficulties was that no gravestone was erected on Father's grave and I was not aware of any visits by her to it. I had a memorial to my father, mother and sister placed in 2010.

My mother had to make a living somehow. With no obvious skills she opened a stocking repair business employing two or three girls who repaired the ladders in the nylon stockings. It did not do well and folded when cheap nylons became freely available. Finally, mother became an auxiliary nurse which she kept up during my dental student days. She had a bad time financially and I cannot forgive my father for leaving her without financial support. One of the first things I did after qualification was to take out a life insurance for £1,500 with profits. In 1956 this was thought to be an adequate sum! It paid out about £16K after 25 years.

I returned to school after the funeral and resumed my studies. Actually, I resumed my activities and filled in the day by doing a bit of work. At some stage I had decided to be a doctor and in discussion with my father he had said that he could not afford to pay for me. Happily, Parliament found the money for the University education for the 5% who made it to these establishments. I don't really know why at an early age I decided upon Medicine. I had wanted to be a Spitfire pilot but the war had ended and I now wore glasses. I have a suspicion my teenage lust for females may have guided me to Medicine which is interesting because when I actually practised gynaecology it proved a sexual turn off. Anyway, after I had re-sat three School Certificate subjects and added three more credits to the original six, the Headmaster agreed I should read biology and chemistry as main subjects and physics and pure maths as subsidiaries for the Higher Schools Certificate. I knew I was weak in all but biology but did not have the sense to understand that the solution lay in my own hands.

Each house had a monitor and sub-monitor for each dormitory. The dormitory monitors were responsible for ensuring the bed areas were tidy and that the beds were presented in a fashion that would meet the approval of the housemaster's inspection. Monitors kept an eye on their charges and could report bad behaviour to the housemaster by using the report book. From the monitors the Head would appoint school monitors who were responsible for much of the day to day organisation. Monitors and sub monitors sat at the head and tail of the long dining tables in Hall and divided out portions of food from the metal trays. One duty that always raised the hair on the back of my neck was to follow a boy who was sleep-walking and guide him back to the dormitory without harm.

My career as a monitor nearly came to an end when I was a sub monitor. Quite unofficially miscreants were 'tanned' by monitors, usually with a slipper. I never was aware of brutality and many boys accepted their punishment as being preferable to being booked. The 'crime' was usually minor, e.g. repeated laughing or talking in prep or after lights out. One night when I was in charge of the dorm when the light out bell sounded, I called 'last one in bed gets a whack.' There was a lot of laughter and shouting as the boys ran around to get into their beds. I gave the last one in one minor blow with whatever was to hand. This bit of fun, as I thought, continued for some time and everybody but the last one seemed to enjoy it. Once I used a coat hanger which to my surprise broke on contact. My surprise came because I had used little force. Anyway, I thought little about this until summoned to see the Headmaster. A mother had written complaining I had struck her son so hard and I had broken a coat hanger on his backside. I was horrified and realised I was in deep trouble. I explained the full circumstances, the fun and laughter and the minimum force used and Kip gave me a severe warning as to my future conduct. It must have worked. I suppose I must have later tanned the odd pupil as was the practice but only for a significant reason.

My second visit to the Headmaster occurred when I was a senior monitor and lunched on the high table. After lunch as we filed out I was surprised to find the Head waiting for me. 'Come to my study,' I was ordered. Kip told me that he had seen me turn up my nose at good food when men were giving their lives to ensure my safety and how dare I insult them and him by doing such a thing. The cause of my distress was the end result of soaking dried marrowfat peas in soda to soften them and then boiling the lot until soft and edible. Alas, one end result of the process was hydrogen sulphide which turned the peas into a stinking mess. The Head had seen me assailed by this smell. 'And another thing,' he said, 'you put too much on your plate because you leave food.' 'No, Headmaster,' I replied, 'my parents brought me up to eat slowly, to chew everything and that results in my still eating when others have cleared their plates.' My explanations must have been reasonable for he did not banish me from his table. To this day I eat slowly compared to others. Some people do not seem to use their teeth and indeed, research shows they do not need to. I wish I could have told the Head that mushy peas remain a favourite of mine with fish and chips. They have found the way to stop them stinking.

I put an average effort into work whilst I indulged myself in sport, the Corps and falling in love with various girls, both local and from Sunderland. As 6th formers we were allowed to walk out with local girls, play tennis with them in the Bowe's Museum which was next door and have visits from home-based lasses who brought picnics with them. I remember the let-down of my first kiss. Somehow Hollywood had made me believe a kiss produced an orchestra and a sensation of floating on clouds. Our combined lack of experience produced nothing at all but wet lips. We had a lot to learn. As each term closed, the holidays were spent with Jimmy Taylor and not my books. The years passed quickly and suddenly we were taking mock exams for the Higher Certificate. I am sure my weaknesses were obvious and I should have got the message. The actual exams were brought forward by several weeks to about 10 days into the summer term. I should have devoted the Easter holidays to swotting but bad habits prevailed over common sense and I was out with Jimmy every day who, of course, didn't have to pass anything as he was to go into the family business. It was only when I returned to school that I got cracking, burning the midnight oil. I remember the dreadful shock I had as I turned over the chemistry paper – I knew immediately I couldn't do it. I had not accrued the basic knowledge to get me out of trouble. For the rest of the term and through the summer vacation, I knew I had failed. The results confirmed my prediction: – Biology – distinction, Chemistry – fail, Physics – pass, Pure Maths – fail. I had failed my Higher!

What followed for me was in effect an acute exogenous depression. The realisation that I was a failure was a humiliation that kept me awake and depressed. I had let my mother, father and myself down and there was no easy solution. I had to let King's College Newcastle know that I had failed and could not take up my place to read Medicine. They suggested Dentistry. The Headmaster at Barney wrote, saying he hoped I would return to provide continuity in the 6th Form for he was certain my distinction meant the fails were an aberration. I could not face going back as a failure and anyway there was no money. If I did not continue in full-time education, I would be called up, so I sought entry to the local Bede Grammar School and was admitted to the final year 6th.

Now 1950, it was the first 'A' level which had replaced the Higher Schools. I had to read three main subjects – biology, chemistry and physics. I played for the School 1st XV and devoted virtually all of my spare time to the books. I can't remember what the teaching was like but I knew my weakness of maths would influence my chemistry and physics so I got

On my 1932 BSA 500 Blue Star motorcycle

stuck into them. I applied and was accepted to read Dentistry, much influenced by the belief I was not clever enough to pass 2nd M.B. and by Dr. Dalgliesh who painted a depressing picture of life in the new NHS. As the exams came close I realised I had neglected the biology and had to work harder. When I took the exams I was aware that I was better informed but weak at the calculations. I didn't dare to turn up to read the results but a phone call from a colleague told me I had the necessary grades. I don't remember ever picking up my results. I then went off to can peas in Blairgowrie for Smedleys.

I drove up to Scotland on a BSA 500 Blue Star motorcycle made in 1932 for which I gave £25. I had no test, no road fund tax or insurance. When I returned I sold the bike for £25. Lucky or stupid?

On my return there was a letter from the medical school at Newcastle offering me a place. My lack of confidence played havoc with my thinking and I had not realised I had now learned how to graft. Now I know I should have dropped Dentistry and gone into Medicine. Then I doubted my ability to pass the exams and, in the absence of wiser advice and a father with whom to talk over my problems, I declined the offer. I would become a dentist and work office hours!

I often wondered later why I was such a lazy lout for so long. As neither parent had higher education they were not in a position to explain to me the pitfalls of idleness. My father's response to a bad school report was a beating, not a discussion on why my report was bad or how I could improve matters. There was little doubt that my friendship with Jimmy Taylor led me into idleness, fun and pleasure, rather than work. Sending me away to Barnard Castle School was a financial sacrifice for my parents – the fees per term in 1944 were £40, I think. This was a significant sum then. There was no doubt I improved considerably and moved up the form to the front row but I did this because I did well with the non-science subjects. I was not dull but certainly had a brain not suited to maths. It was unfortunate that the masters during the war were elderly but from 1945 onwards, as they were replaced by those coming back from the war, nobody grabbed me to tell me to pull myself together. It was unfortunate also that the Higher Schools exams were brought forward by a month to just after Easter vac. I am sure if I had spent that vacation revising instead of playing around with Jimmy I would have got away with it.

Would I have had a similar career without this major lesson at 18? I never failed another exam, either under-graduate or post-graduate, and I learned to plan my career path with specific targets for five year periods. I made sure I got there by hard work. I think I made the best of a bad job in the end but only after a really life-changing event and failure and a wasted year.

The failure of that exam left its mark on me. For years after, even after retirement, I would dream that I was having trouble working for, or getting to, or sitting exams. I would struggle to wake up to the realisation that I was already, or had been, a consultant and that my anxieties were needless. Variations of this theme have occurred in my dreams since I was 18. I don't know what the psychiatrist would make of that but I believe that failure left its mark on me and made me determined I would not fail to achieve a goal for lack of effort.

4 University Dental Training

I became a dental student in Newcastle-Upon-Tyne Medical School in October 1951, entering the 2nd year of a six year course. The 2nd BDS included the anatomy of the head, neck and thorax, human physiology and histology of normal human tissue. Initially, most of us were apprehensive of dissecting human cadavers but we rapidly descended into the usual dissecting room language and tricks led by our ex-National Service colleagues with their practised barrack room humour. A favourite was to over-pack the shelves of a fridge cupboard used by a female group with partially dissected bodies. When they opened the door!

I enjoyed this intensive course and the several areas of knowledge that opened up for me. I cannot remember wearing gloves for dissection which was a big leap up from my early attempts on the earthworm, dogfish and frog for Higher School Certificate. Even though we lacked any knowledge of the application of anatomy to patient care there was considerable satisfaction in dissection, in passing the repetitive vivas and understanding the physiology of the body.

The anatomy theatre was on the top floor of the Medical School, access being by stairs. Before long, I found it increasingly difficult to climb them and had to stop several times. As I panted for breath, a female lecturer passed me and asked, 'What is the matter?' After I told her of my increasing weakness she made arrangements for me to be seen by a physician in the Royal Victoria Infirmary across the road. I found myself lying on a bed embarrassingly surrounded by the consultant and a number of medical students. I was happy to learn it was not leukaemia and that I would recover from glandular fever without recourse to unpleasant treatment and I must have done so. I wondered which girl had given it to me! It was the so called 'kissing disease' of the young. If it was I had passed it on.

The 2nd BDS exam had a regular high failure rate and in order to avoid that experience again I started to work hard several months before the exam. In the event everything went well even to having a distinction viva in anatomy; unfortunately, this extended into the brain about which I knew very little. However, I passed and had three free months for some holiday and a chance to earn money. I did several jobs, including dry cleaning eiderdowns and taxi driving and it was wonderful to have a few pound notes of my own in my pocket.

I had been awarded a County major scholarship or grant by Sunderland County Borough Council - £165 per annum, paid in three instalments on receipt of proof of my continued presence in college in addition to college fees. Each £55 provided for my travel, books and other expenses and my poor mother, left destitute by my father's early death, tried to make a living to keep us both in our rented house. I lived at home in Sunderland to keep my mother company whilst enjoying her cooking and her care. I continued to play rugby and some cricket in Sunderland and travelled backwards and forwards each working day to Newcastle. It was hardly a University experience, but from this distance I can see we were a lucky generation to have such financial support.

Most mornings I got a lift in an MG sports car, driven by a same year colleague Dennis Clarke, a son of a local dentist. Dennis had the patience of Job for I was usually a few minutes late arriving in Fawcett Street where he waited for me. (Have a life-time problem getting up in the mornings and getting to bed at night.) We picked up another colleague, Jimmy Thompson, on the way and the three of us sat on two seats without seat belts which paid Dennis' petrol costs. I have a scar in the middle of my forehead to remind me of one of those trips on a winter morning when we skidded on ice and hit a bridge parapet. My forehead contacted the electric motor on top of the windscreen, impacting its handle in the skin. The blood spurted. When seat belts came in several years later I was involved in treating facial injuries. I was a convert to them long before they were compulsory. I returned home by bus if Dennis was otherwise engaged. Inevitably, I was asleep before the bus crossed the Tyne Bridge and frequently woke up in fog from a sea fret cloaking the coast. The North East could be very uncomfortable.

King's College sited in Newcastle-Upon-Tyne was a constituent college of Durham University. King's trained the doers and Durham the thinkers. The Dental School was part of the medical faculty and as such I wore the faculty badge on my blazer though I did use a dental scarf. I felt happier if people thought I was a medical student. I was beginning to have serious doubts about my choice of Dentistry and after passing the 2nd BDS I applied with another colleague to do the combined medical and dental course which was included in the University literature. We were unsuccessful because 'there were not enough to justify the extra work for the college authorities'.

The new academic year saw me entering Sutherland Dental School for the 3rd BDS course. The Dean of the School, Robert, later Sir Robert, Bradlaw, was a domineering bachelor with a personality; he was qualified in both Medicine, and Dentistry. It took considerable courage to argue with him. The BDS Course he had created was six years long, the same as Medicine and he sought equality between these disciplines in several other ways. The wearing of academic dress was compulsory for all lectures and formal occasions and he insisted upon a reasonable standard of dress and behaviour. In this we were usually different from most other undergraduates in the other faculties.

The six year course was too long and should have been five. The third year was a big turn off and profligate in time wasting. The dental mechanics course was the principal culprit; a few weeks of this would have sufficed. I remember carving plaster teeth in order to reproduce the classic dental restorations and we were introduced to dental histology. It was a terrible waste of time and a great relief to complete. Several colleagues spent most of the day playing cards which I am sure was a better use of their time. After the 3rd BDS exam was passed, I drove with my mother in her little Morris Eight down to London to visit my sister. During our stay we met and lunched with a commercial friend of my late father. David Cadwallader was Chairman of CAV, a firm that manufactured components for diesel engines. After lunch at the RAC Club he took me to one side and was complimentary about my personality, telling me it was just what his firm required. He offered to employ me as a management and sales trainee at £1K a year. These were riches beyond my dreams. I don't know if I declined his offer immediately but I did realise I would have to leave King's without a Degree and it would have been wasted time and effort. I would also have to do National Service. I declined his offer and another missed life-changing opportunity was added to my list.

After the 3rd BDS we had to prepare for the three years of clinical studies. We had to provide dental instruments and a portable cabinet in which to keep them and several white coats. This was a major investment and involved the purchase of much second-hand equipment and books from the newly qualified dentists. Money was always tight and more than once I had to prioritise between the purchasing of a pair of underpants or a shoe repair. Clinical students no longer enjoyed academic vacations for, although the lectures were limited to University terms, patient care and clinical practice continued. The clinical years consisted of lectures in the morning and clinical work in the afternoon with the reverse in the next year. This allowed the dental students to have sufficient dental units and patients at one time. We were gradually trained to give injections of local analgesic, perform dental extractions, dental fillings and denture provision. Everything we did was supervised and checked at each stage by qualified staff. A chit was signed on completion after the procedure and points were awarded accordingly for the several procedures. A minimum target of points had to be completed before being allowed to sit the final examinations.

The 1950s were pre-fluoride toothpaste and the lack of dental consciousness and dental disease was manifest. We rapidly developed our skills for there was no shortage of patients. Dental extractions were performed with local or general anaesthetic, the latter being common as many patients were frightened by the needle. Students were allocated to dental extractions under local anaesthesia or general dental anaesthesia and the giving of general anaesthesia. I particularly enjoyed general anaesthesia, as it was 'medical' and the anaesthetists who trained us were consultant anaesthetists. Almost all anaesthetic agents were gaseous as intra-venous Penothal was then used only for in-patients. The presence of two strong male porters was essential and each adult patient was held in the dental chair by a leather strap. The weakness of the anaesthetic agents produced cerebral irritation which could result in enormous struggles by a male and even the occasional female. The porters were there to physically control them. We were strongly advised never to straighten the clothing of ladies before they could do so themselves in case they believed they had been assaulted as consciousness returned. Several cases of alleged assault in these circumstances had ended in the courts.

There was a considerable skill involved in gaseous dental anaesthesia for it was all too easy to precipitate oxygen lack and deep cyanosis with potential brain damage. Because of its medical emphasis I looked forward to my allocated sessions. Unlike today, when dental extractions are relatively rare, I soon became expert in dental extraction. The expression 'pulling teeth' was highly misleading. It is impossible to pull a tooth out of normal bone. Extraction requires that the forceps' blades be pushed as far as possible on the tooth root before gripping the whole tooth to apply leverage and rotation compatible with its anatomy. The lower jaw of the unconscious patient had to be supported by the other hand to protect the airway. Strength was a factor and the girls were not always well suited. If a tooth broke the roots were removed by the supervising house surgeon.

We did not wear gloves and were constantly washing our hands. If they were not well dried it was easy to develop a painful rash. It is almost impossible now to imagine the rank stench of many patients' mouths resulting from their foul oral hygiene. The compensation for us was clinical experience. Years later, on a lecture tour of the States, I watched a senior dental surgeon in a teaching hospital preparing the patient for a simple dental extraction with full theatre draping and sedation before spending about five minutes fighting a premolar tooth until it fell out from exhaustion. It would have taken me about five seconds. I expect the lack of experience of dental extraction today will produce something similar in this country.

Saturday morning in the dental extraction clinic was usually fun;

Dental Students. From left: Bell, Davidson, Clarke, Hopkins. Behind: Phillip. The Dean Professor Robert Bradlaw insisted his students dressed like professional men and wore academic gowns at lectures. Here seen on the way to memorial service for King George VIth.

the patients were usually manual and industrial workers. These men who were otherwise as tough as old boots were often scared of the 'needle'. If the waiting room was still crowded near midday and we had to get away to play our various games, we would get one of the nurses to scream. That usually got rid of those not in severe pain so that we could finish on time.

By the early 1950s dental local analgesia had been improved by the substitution of reusable hypodermic needles, that had to be re-sharpened, by fine bore disposable injection needles that were very sharp and relatively painless. The local analgesic solution came in 2cc cartridges with a syringe to match instead of bottles. We developed the skills of giving relatively painless injections though many patients still remained apprehensive. Injections were by local infiltration or by regional blocks which desensitised areas of the face and jaws. The most difficult injection to learn was the mandibular block which requires the insertion of the needles at the back of the mouth and its penetration in three different angles to inject around the mandibular nerve. It was quite easy to lose the sense of where the needle tip was and every now and again a student would inject into the parotid gland causing a temporary partial or complete facial paralysis. It was not unknown for the needle to emerge through the skin posterior to the lower jaw and squirt onto the wall! Not every student developed their skills at the same pace.

After the start of the fifth year, I had become the Student President and had to earn money in order to go to a Congress in Malmo, Sweden. I got a job as a passenger porter at the main railway station in Sunderland on the back shift – 4 till midnight. It was the station where I got on the train to go to boarding school and where, to my amazement, a German bomb had blown a goods wagon out of the station roof in the 1940s. We were over-manned, working only when a train arrived. I found it easy to be pleasant to old ladies when helping them with their bags and I acquired good tips. At the end of the week I was told by my fellow porters that all tips had to be pooled but when I found I had acquired as much as the rest of them put together I declined their invitation. The following week they complained to the foreman and I was promoted to be a parcel porter – paid a little more but no tips. The bastards!

My first job on the shift was to sweep the platform so using a huge brush I swept the platform depositing the litter on the track, as the permanent staff had done the previous week. The Inspector shot out of the staff room. 'Don't do that!' he cried. 'Sweep it into heaps and put it in the bin.' This I proceeded to do but then I could not find either a shovel or a bin so I went into the room where they were playing poker and reported this to the Inspector. 'Come with me,' he said picking up the brush. He started to sweep the centre of the platform, brush at an angle. He turned and brushed back, at an angle, so that the dust was moved towards the platform edge. Finally, he brushed along the edge so that the dirt fell unobtrusively onto the track. 'There,' he said in all seriousness. 'Tricks in every trade; don't sweep directly onto the track.' I now knew why there were no shovels or bins. The rest of my job was to bring parcels from the store and put them into the guard's carriage and take off all parcels for Sunderland and put them in the store. In between trains there was poker. I discovered I made enough money to replace the tips, even though I was not a proven poker player.

After a couple of weeks I was promoted to be a leading porter and in charge of the back shift. My fellow workers included permanent staff who complained to the Station Master about being passed over for a casual worker. I held my post. Several porters, like me, were casual workers. One of my jobs was to cut up toilet rolls on a guillotine to stop them being stolen and thrown at Roker Park football ground. It was strong, non-absorbent paper soaked in Izal. I gave a porter a heap of this and told him to put it in the toilets. He returned from visiting about 25 toilets with a similar sized wad of paper explaining that he had put a sheet in each one! Another bright spark reported a constantly running water closet. I told him to lock the door until the plumber could get there. When we realised the porter was missing we went in search of him and found him locked inside the toilet. Presumably he proposed to stay there until we found the plumber. These were the days of full employment and staff quality was thin.

After six weeks, I had earned enough money to go to Sweden and enjoy myself. There I met a Swedish dental student called Eva whose family name appeared on many large construction cranes. She wanted me to marry her but it was too quick for me even though the family was loaded. I had had three love affairs during my time at Dental School: Eileen who had broken my young heart, Joy with whom I spent two happy years before I broke hers, and June who attracted me considerably but who wanted somebody with money and not just potential. I was not yet ready for marriage, preferring the pleasures inherent in women, and I needed to make money.

During these three clinical years, our practice progressed to include the provision of bridges, gold inlays, crowns and dentures. Gold inlays required considerable skill and several done by earlier students had to be replaced. We were supposed to hand in the gold but it was easy to use to make ornaments for girlfriends. Years later I made my wife's wedding ring using these dental skills. In addition to practical work, we were examined in general and oral pathology, general and oral medicine, dental jurisprudence, ethics and professionalism, but never received instruction on how to run a practice. With a few exceptions, I had a poor regard for most of the dental academics who seemed to me to specialise in mediocrity. Bradlaw appeared to collect them but perhaps the early NHS enabled dentists to make so much money that only those incapable of such hard work became academics. Over the years this unscientific opinion of mine did not change much. It is significant that the 5th year course of general medicine and surgery, which included ward based clinical teaching with a professional examination at its end, was for me the most enjoyable of my course. This was a portent of things to come.

My course drew to a close. I had developed many of the skills of a dental practitioner but was fed up of poverty. The final exams were a mixture of clinical practice and written papers with several viva voces which I passed, along with the majority of students. Our degrees were presented in Durham Castle and we proceeded in our gowns and hoods from the Cathedral cloisters. My mother was there to share the day. It was the only time during the five years that I felt I was at University. My undergraduate days were over. I was 24. I sold my books and instruments to a new year of clinical students and determined I would make money and not sit another exam. I do not remember how much I was overdrawn at the bank but it was not a lot.

5 First Job in Dental Practice and Increasing Disillsionment.

Near the end of my undergraduate course I had a medical examination for National Service and, to my disgust, a combination of flat feet and nasal rhinitis resulted in a medical Grade C. Just before I qualified the Government announced only Grades A & B would be called up. So, despite still playing a variety of ball games, with average skills and being the senior CCF cadet at school, I found myself spared two years that I was actually looking forward to. I had fancied being commissioned and travelling the world. However, I now had an unexpected bonus of two years.

I found a short term post as an assistant dental surgeon near Hartlepool. It was a blood and vulcanite practice owned by a dentist who had gained access to the Dentists Register without University training. Most of these practitioners had been dental mechanics who had strayed into making dentures and dental extractions. After the 1921 Act of Parliament this became illegal but in 1956 there were still many of them providing limited care for the working class patients and making considerable sums of money in the early days of the NHS. Outside of the middle classes dental consciousness hardly existed, so it was common to find edentulous adults in their 20s. I was horrified to be requested to remove reasonable teeth from young women whose wedding present from their father was to be a dental clearance and a set of dentures. I refused to do this and attempted to persuade these women to look after their mouths. I did not doubt they would find somebody to do their bidding but they did not realise that the end result of this practice was a prematurely aged forty year old who could not wear a lower denture comfortably but had to put them in to answer the front door or attend social events. Thank goodness such wedding presents must be comparatively rare today, thanks to fluoride toothpaste and advertising. My principal memory of this job was that, because I was newly qualified, I gave the general anaesthetics every morning for eight to twelve patients who were to have dental extractions. I enjoyed giving these anaesthetics even though I was acutely aware of their potential danger to patients. At that time it was accepted that general anaesthesia was part of dentistry and many thousands of anaesthetics were given with a varying degree of skill. As with all procedures there were complications, some of them fatal. General anaesthetics in dental practice are no longer permitted.

Chloroform was no longer used because of its several dangers, including liver damage, and young children were induced by dripping ether on a mask, sometimes with additional ethyl chloride. Once anaesthetised, the dentist placed the gag in the mouth, opened it, inserted the throat pack and whipped out the teeth before the patient started to recover. Another technique involved breaking a small phial of vinyl ether (Vinesthene) onto a sponge inside a metal cylinder attached to a rubber bladder on one end and a face mask with a non-return valve on the other. The child breathed this vapour in and out and rapidly became anaesthetised. Again, the surgeon had to get a move on; at least these techniques avoided oxygen lack and long term damage. Older children were induced in a similar manner to adults but, hopefully, with a greater percentage of oxygen. Many patients vomited on recovery if they had disobeyed instructions regarding eating and drinking beforehand, which was life threatening if they inhaled the vomit. The chair had to rapidly be tilted backwards and strong suction used to clear the throat. Frequently, the dentist gave the anaesthetic and removed the teeth using an unqualified dental nurse to hold the head. Not only were techniques inherently dangerous but the quality of the anaesthetists varied enormously. Some hospital consultant anaesthetists worked in dental surgeries and some GPs and GDPs specialised in dental anaesthesia; some GPs gave the odd anaesthetic and were as dangerous as the technique. It was common for a GP to tell their patients who presented with facial swelling to go to their dentist and he would come to give the anaesthetic, for which he would be paid. One such experience occurred to me in Cambridge when the GP turned on the machine and watched the patient go blue. When I told him oxygen was required he did not know what to do. I ended up moving the dials and doing the extractions. All the GP did was hold the jaw, so when he asked for his money I told him where to go and never come back. He didn't press me for the cash.

The foregoing will have highlighted how dangerous dental anaesthesia

My Triumph Roadster

was, but that was the state of the art in which I believed I was quite skilled and enjoyed. It must be remembered that millions of dental anaesthetics were given in dental practices with very few fatalities resulting. We shall never know the real extent of brain damage. If you remember, people walked in off the street and then walked out a short while later often with their mouth full of blood; it was quite barbaric. This was the essence of my first job, happily lasting only a few weeks.

I successfully applied for a post of Assistant Dental Surgeon in a practice at 2 Hills Road, Cambridge. I believed a job in Cambridge should be fun and so it proved. The dental practice was a disappointment, however, for the assistant's surgery was not equipped with the modern air rotor, the lightweight turbine that was so much easier and quicker to use than the electric motor driven drill; this was heavy and left me exhausted by the end of the day. The boss, who had qualified at Guy's, was delightfully out of date and hardly commercial. The practice manager, a Mrs. Rayner, a widow in her late 40s, and my dental nurse, a farmer's daughter in her late teens made the job bearable. This girl was competent, attractive and fun. She had a boyfriend and I knew I had to behave professionally and keep off but there was an increasing awareness that there was a mutual attraction developing. Thank God this was before the days of sexual harassment. It was a good job I left before matters got out of control!

There were other compensations. I had digs on the opposite side of Parker's Piece which was an easy walk to Hills Road and covered by cricket pitches in the summer. My landlady, in her 60s, was a heavy smoker and was as thin as a rake. She gave me breakfast and an evening meal which I took with her and her long suffering husband Jim. She did not object to my having visitors in my front bed sitting room.

1956 was still the aftermath of the Suez Crisis and petrol was rationed. As prices on second hand cars had dropped considerably, I was able to buy my first car with which I fell deeply in love. It was a black Triumph Roadster, 2 litre, with a bench seat in the front and dicky seats in the back, a canvas hood and two huge headlamps. The gear change was on the steering column and the car body made from aluminium. Delightfully, my farming patients used to give me paraffin coupons with which I bought petrol so the rationing was not a problem. I drove up to Sunderland a couple of times to see my mother and take her out in it. I met a girl called Pat who was dark headed, vivacious and a Roman Catholic. In her early 20s, Pat was full of fun, willing and available but, not for the last time, her religion was a problem for me. My mother had brought me up to distrust Catholicism, even though she was a high church Anglican and had sent my sister to St. Antony's, a Catholic school in Sunderland.

There was another dental practice around the corner in Lensfield Road. I met the owner who told me a relative of his, Margaret Harrison, was his practice manager and that she too came from Sunderland. Did she have a daughter called Ann I asked ? 'Yes' he replied. Some little time later I met them both and, after a 14 year gap, renewed our acquaintance. During the war the Government had encouraged people to stay at home during summer holidays. To entertain those who did, shows and concerts were arranged for their pleasure and one such was Merry England played and sung on an apron stage round the bandstand in Barnes Park in the summer open air. I was to be first Page, Ann second and another lad third. I had a speaking part. I remember telling a servant, 'Take thyself hence. I like not the proximity of thy face.' This always got a laugh from the audience for reasons I never understood. Ann was a year or so older than me and all three pages had lots of fun during rehearsals, playing under the apron stage. Ann's mother, the lead soprano, was Queen Elizabeth, so we were always under supervision — well not quite. One afternoon Ann, obviously feeling the pressures of impending womanhood, asked me if I had ever seen what a lady had under her knickers. No I said, so we reached an immediate agreement to change this. This was my first experience of pubic hair and my first touch of a thickening chest, later to be a breast. It was also my first erection resulting from a girl's hand. I think I was 10 or 11 for I went away to school when I was 12, in 1944.

Such innocent pleasure! When we met again 14 years later we both remembered and laughed about the experience but could not follow it up as Ann had a long term, much older, boyfriend who was a producer director of the amateur Cambridge Arts Theatre. It was through him that I was introduced to the group of players and had parts in two productions at the Arts Theatre. I played Samuel Pepys in the Diary of an MP and had to wear a cushion around my midriff. I was miscast.

The winter in Cambridge was damp and cold but compensated by the summer, drinking beer outdoors at Trumpington, watching cricket at Fennes and having the hood down on the Roadster. Cambridge, as a University City, was everything Newcastle was not and I delighted in the atmosphere. Something was wrong however. I was exhausted by the end of the day and on several occasions when I had really done good work on a patient, my reward was to be told — Thank God, I don't have to see you again for some time! It was difficult not to reply in kind. As a bachelor it seemed I paid nearly everything I earned in Income Tax and it was not long before I began to feel disillusioned.

6 Dental Practice in Rhodesia

I had been in Cambridge a year when I read an advert in the British Dental Journal for an assistant in Salisbury, Southern Rhodesia. The principal was in the UK and I arranged to meet him. Eric Wiley, a middle-aged Leeds graduate, was a delightful man who painted an attractive picture of life in Southern Rhodesia. He offered and I accepted. Six weeks later I landed in Salisbury without my Roadster which I had sold for the £350 I had paid for it, petrol rationing having eased. I went up home to bid farewell to my mother. I still remember her crying as the train drew out and was unaware, in my excitement, of what I was doing to her. With my father dead and my sister in the South, she was alone and short of money. Oh, if only we could repair the damage we cause in our youth.

I flew out to Salisbury in a BOAC Britannia, in two hour hops to Rome, then Khartoum, where the heat off the runway at night hit one as we left the aircraft and where I first saw people lying asleep on the concrete all around the airport building. Moths flew everywhere. I think we then flew to Entebbe and thence to Salisbury. It took about 24 hours and we arrived in the early afternoon. I was met by my new boss and taken straight to the car racing circuit at Marandellas. It was very hot and I was wearing a thick suit. I was plied with cold Lion Lager and, as the altitude was 6,000 feet and I had not slept for 24 hours, I passed out.

Until I found somewhere to live I stayed with Eric and his wife in their new house outside Salisbury and I was introduced to the concept of African servant boys, be it cookhouse, garden or 'go for'. I became used to the short interval between sunset and darkness and a quality of life new to me. There were downsides, like insects, mosquitoes and snakes in outbuildings, but it wasn't long before I dressed, behaved and drank like most expats. I rented an apartment in Salisbury and was lucky to find a cook/houseboy called Sixpence who was a wonder. His family probably lived miles away in the bush. He washed, cleaned and cooked for me. Giving dinner parties involved giving him money to buy food and the food appeared. It was too easy. He was delightful.

The social life for an expat could be described as racy. Parties of all varieties were from formal to pyjamas and with so many young single people with time and money on their hands it was not possible to be bored. I bought a VW Beetle which was ideal for strip and dirt roads when driven flat out to even out the corrugations. Unfortunately, at night this could result in driving into a large animal or another car and there were repeated reports of road accidents. Snakes on the road required the applying of brakes in order to skid over and kill them, otherwise they could be whipped up onto the underside of the car where they could stay in a bad temper until you stopped. If you then shut them in the garage there could be a problem when you next opened its door.

The population of Southern Rhodesia in 1958 seemed to me to be at peace with itself; undoubtedly the whites ran the show and in the main regarded this as their right. Whilst many Afrikaners held the African in low esteem, the majority of Brits did not appear to abuse them. Public services to the African were well run and staffed competently with reasonable health and education provision. The Rhodesian African appeared to be much happier than those in South Africa and crossing Beit Bridge into the Republic introduced one to a sullen population and quite different atmosphere. The Federation of Southern and Northern Rhodesia and Nyasaland was governed by Sir Roy Welensky, an ex-heavyweight boxer, whilst Southern Rhodesia had its own government headed by Sir Edgar Whitehead. There was a black Postmaster General in the Government and all in all the future seemed set for prosperity and stability.

The dental practice had three partners and two assistants. Eric Wiley, in his 40s, was a jovial senior partner, taking life as it comes and Peter Macdonald was a large well-built South African extravert and ex-rugby player. He had a beautiful wife and young family. The third partner, a colourless individual and Guy's man, did not impress himself upon my consciousness, nor did his similar wife. The other assistant was a young married mother with children.

I enjoyed working in Salisbury. The equipment was modern; the patients paid for their treatment and appreciated what you did. I gave most of the dental general anaesthetics and did minor surgicals. I was paid a good percentage of my total take and before long was earning good money. In a backroom inhabited by the dental mechanics there was an old wooden dental chair. African patients could, for a small fee of about 50p, have a dental extraction with local anaesthesia rather than go to Government dental clinics. I soon appreciated that the African jaw had a large proportion of reinforced concrete. I was called one day to see an African with an infected, impacted wisdom tooth. I should have sent him away but I did explain it would require a surgical removal. He asked me to proceed. When I picked up the syringe to inject local anaesthetic, he refused it saying he was a member of a Christian sect who believed pain was sent by God for their good. It took me ages to remove the bone and section the tooth so that I could remove it in the separate pieces. The patient remained mouth wide open, uncomplaining, immovable, sweat free and totally cooperative. I was overwhelmed by admiration for him, his stoicism and his belief but I was soaked in my own sweat resulting from the hard work and my lack of experience.

Many of our patients came from the farming communities miles away. Farming incomes were intimately related to the sale of their products, so those in tobacco received the bulk of their money annually. This resulted in some of them paying their bills once a year. By accepting this we did them a favour which they often repaid by including an invitation to a party at their farm when they paid their bill. Cars from near and far would arrive to find the whole farm prepared to party. There would be a large hole in the ground full of red hot embers around which were mounds of meat and sausage with tanks of lager, a swimming pool and music from a band or records. It did not take long for formality to disappear, particularly when darkness came. There was a lot of testosterone and at the party's end, we slept in mosquito net covered hammocks slung in empty barns strongly smelling of tobacco. What went on inside some of those mosquito nets left little to the imagination.

A different wild life was available in the game parks. Peter Macdonald agreed to take me to the Kruger National Park. We filled the front of my Beetle with Lion lager and sun-dried buffalo meat or biltong and drove down to cross Beit Bridge into South Africa. When we arrived in the park there was a variety of accommodation in several camps. Rondarvels were round, thatched stone huts with a restaurant in a bigger one, whilst in other camps ex-army Bell tents and camp beds sufficed. My coldest night ever was in a Bell tent with one blanket. It had been warm sitting by the fire drinking lager but when I went to sleep the temperature dropped to below freezing and I woke up shivering uncontrollably with ice on the outside of the tent. With sunrise I soon warmed up.

My first view of the many wild animals, hitherto seen only in pictures, filled me with delight. Africa has the unique smell of the dust from the red earth and to lie awake at night listening to the call of a lion or hippo, to see the glow of huge bush fires in the night sky, or listen to the sounds of native drumming in the distance was atmospheric. It is a different, wonderful world. A huge world with stars seemingly near enough to hold. I wonder if anyone who has grown up accustomed to the repetitive yet wonderful TV images of wildlife can experience the same excitement and wonder of my first experiences of wild life in Africa. I visited game parks in Portuguese East Africa, Rhodesia and Kenya. Each was a wonderful experience.

Although the social life of Salisbury was varied, culture was in short supply. I gained membership of the Salisbury Sports Club after a few months and played golf with pungent tobacco waste spread over the grass to encourage green growth. Of course, there was a 'boy' to carry the clubs. Despite the threat of snakes in the rough they were shoeless and in the habit of making bets with each other on a potential winner. If their man's ball lay in a bad position in the rough they would pick up the ball in their toes and place it so that the boss could play it when they came up. It was almost unknown to lose a ball. How so many white South Africans became world class golfers in such circumstances is surprising.

Visits from professional theatre companies were relatively rare so the amateur theatre was strong. I joined the Salisbury Rep and was in the production of the Diary of Ann Frank, playing Mr. Van Daan, the man who stole the bread. Again, I had to wear false weight and colour my hair grey. Mrs. Van Daan was a comely 40ish woman with whom I had to share a stage bed about two feet wide. To avoid falling off, I had to hold onto her. As we got to know each other better so did my hold and our closeness and this in front of an audience. Thank God for the blanket covering us. Amateur theatre is also full of testosterone. There was a large Jewish population in Rhodesia. As we lay in our two foot wide bed, we could hear the weeping from the audience, some of whom must have survived the Holocaust and all its horror. The long term benefits of amateur theatre became obvious later when I started to lecture. No one in the back seats of the largest lecture hall ever complained that they could not hear me. Nobody went to sleep either.

In the high voltage social life of Rhodesia, it was relatively easy to find a girlfriend. Marriage did not figure predominantly in my thoughts at this time. I was not the product of an obvious love marriage and I had the picture in my mind, planted by my mother, of the sort of girl I should marry. Slim, beautiful, intelligent, well-spoken and mannered and Protestant – very middle class. Not easy to find. I met a Rhodesian girl who was rather plain in appearance and dress, but I fell for her voice. However hard I tried I made little progress with her. I knew I was being stupid, falling for a voice but her constant rejection of me stimulated my interest. I was not short of compensations but I cannot now remember all the individuals. A girl I do remember was a patient of mine and a Theatre Sister at the African Hospital at Harari. Elizabeth was a beautiful girl about my age. After we had been out a few times and the seeds of romance had started to germinate, she told me she was a Roman Catholic. I had a long standing mistrust of Catholicism and rejected the insistence that all children of a mixed marriage must be Catholic. I should have discussed this with her but was too fixed in my ideas to do so. She was very keen and I remember Elizabeth with regret. However, marriage was not my first priority and could have scuppered my future career.

In Rhodesia, I renewed acquaintance with one of the first loves of my life, Eileen Dawson née Williams with whom I had been smitten in my early 20s. We had been to the musical South Pacific together at Drury Lane and most of the love songs in that show still remain in my head. She broke my heart, married David Dawson and they left Sunderland to settle in Rhodesia where he owned/managed a hotel restaurant near Salisbury. We became friends again, but only socially. Seven years later we met again in the UK but her magic for me had gone by then.

One morning I was working on a patient when a 'boy' brought in a telegram. 'Sister dead; letter follows.' I still remember the shock, the weakness, the helplessness. After making the patient comfortable, I requested and was given the day off. I did not know what to do. Overseas telephone communication had to be booked and I could not ring my mother, nor do I remember doing so. For some reason I went instead to the Anglican Salisbury Cathedral and requested to speak to a priest. I waited and waited and finally an obviously irritated gentleman arrived enquiring what he could do for me. When I told him what had happened he obviously did not consider this important enough to delay him. After a couple of sentences containing the words 'the Lord giveth, the Lord taketh away', he was off taking with him my last vestige of belief in his religion. In retrospect, I acknowledge it was unfair to blame him but I needed more than a glib comment and did not get it. Irene, who had become depressed following several spontaneous abortions, had put her head in a coal gas oven and turned it on. This was her last act of grand theatre and the most unwelcome. She left a girl child of two years, a husband and a mother who grieved until she too died.

I realised I would have to bring my mother out to Southern Rhodesia if I stayed. I was undecided what to do. I had been offered a full partnership in the practice which I was reluctant to accept. I missed the British seasonal weather, the pubs, and Europe. Above all, one day I realised I could not face the prospect of filling teeth for the rest of my life. I yearned to do something that satisfied my wish to be more involved in patient care and do something that patients appreciated. My mother's isolation and my professional dissatisfaction brought matters to a head. Quite coincidentally, an advert appeared in the British Dental Journal for a Senior House Officer post in Nottingham General Hospital to work in oral surgery and on maxillo-facial injuries. I applied by letter air mail and was appointed by return of post – a very unusual mechanism. I handed in my resignation which the partners reluctantly accepted. My last month also produced my best month's salary as several courses of treatment were concluded. I booked my passage home by ship from Beira on the British India line. Going home this way took me up the East African Ports, through the newly reopened Suez Canal and thence to England. I brought my VW home with me. It was a wonderful trip, full of the smells of spices and the sights of African and Arabian culture.

7 Nottingham, My First Oral Surgery Job

Tom Battersby, the Consultant oral Surgeon at Nottingham, was a remarkable man who became an influential father figure to me. He was the son of a successful Nottinghamshire dentist, educated in a public school which left him with an upper crust accent and an upper middle class existence – riding to hounds, amateur artist of note, a man of culture. He was also an excellent clinician and surgeon. He had been an army dental officer in the war involved in the treatment of facial injury. In the NHS after 1948 there were a few consultant dental/oral surgeons most of whom were ex-service but few had acquired a proper training. If they were employed in Plastic and Jaw Units, they were usually subordinate to the plastic surgeons. Tom was qualified in Dentistry but he had acquired the new FDS, RCS, being one of the first three successful candidates along with Norman Rowe and Homer Killey. In Nottingham the Plastic Unit was in the City Hospital headed by a bumptious, heavy drinking David Wyn Williams. Nottingham General, where Tom had his base and beds, had the A & E Department. This enabled him to do much of the maxillofacial trauma that the plastic surgeons regarded as theirs but were unable to do without dental support. I met Tom for the first time in his private rooms not far from the hospital. He was ebullient, jovial and gave me a generous welcome. I liked him immediately.

That same day I assisted him with an operating list on which there was a patient with a depressed fracture of a cheekbone. Tom demonstrated the Gillies lift to me which involved the insertion of an elevator through an incision on the temple to below and under the depressed cheekbone. Once in position, a rolled bandage was placed as a fulcrum so that the elevator could lever the cheekbone up into its correct position. Usually as the cheekbone was lifted the several bone fragments impacted into each other and retained their position provided pressure on the area postoperatively was avoided. Reducing this fracture appeared a simple procedure and it was possible to determine the accurate reduction of the orbital skeleton by palpitation with one's fingers. Tom mentioned if a fracture was unstable, the antrum was packed with cotton gauze strip in dipped Whitehead's varnish to hold the fracture, the orbital skeleton and orbital floor in position from below.

This operating list exposed me to oral surgery that I had never seen before. Wisdom teeth were surgically removed quickly and simply. Instruments of which I had no knowledge were manifest. The operating theatre was staffed by efficient nurses. The anaesthetists inserted airways into the tracheal wind pipe via the nose. It was a new exciting world.

In 1958 junior hospital staff were called by lights. Each clinic, ward or theatre had the same four colours in a tube. Each member of staff had a colour code, when your lights came on you went to the nearest telephone. Early that same night my lights came on in the Doctors' Mess. I had an acute heart race with apprehension. I was wanted in Casualty. There I found a man with the signs and symptoms of a depressed cheekbone. After radiographic examination I telephoned the boss and after describing the injury said I would like to do it. 'OK, call me if you need to; he replied. When the patient was ready, an Anaesthetics SHO and I

T G Battersby (Tom)

went to theatre. My first, and admittedly small, skin incision in the shaved temple went well. I found the temporal fascia, incised it and got the elevator down the anatomical plane between it and underlying muscle to beneath the cheekbone. All well – the elevation was successful but when I lifted up the cheekbone it seemed to relapse as I eased the pressure. 'It's unstable,' I thought. I remembered what Tom told me and made an intraoral incision in the cheek sulcus to find the fracture line. I also found a blood vessel for blood welled up obliterating my view. Neither suction nor my vain attempts to identify the source were successful. It seemed to me the patient was bleeding to death. I did not know then that firm pressure from a pack for a few minutes, whilst we talked about the weather, would have done the trick. I wanted the floor to open up and for me to escape. I thought my career had ended before it had begun! Happily, the bleeding slowly stopped itself and I completed the antral packing which was probably not required. I was learning the hard way. Next morning with his cheekbone in good position we discharged the patient.

It was some time before my lights going on did not increase my heart rate. I never knew what awaited me. We took facial injuries from Derby, Grantham and Mansfield as well as Nottingham and the surrounding areas. Seat belts were unknown; windscreens were not laminated; motor cyclists singularly or in groups crashed frequently without the benefit of crash helmets. One consultant and one SHO, we put their faces back together again. Additionally, there was a constant supply of bleeding tooth sockets and faces and necks full of pus from dental abscesses. There was much satisfaction incising and draining these, inserting a gloved finger to explore the nooks and crannies of the soft tissue cavity. The old surgical saying 'Where there is pus let it out' was proven many times. I doubt if such abscesses are seen today.

Weekends produced fractures from fights and rugby. Tom taught me to open up and expose a mandibular fracture through a neck incision and reduce and fix it with a metal plate and screws originally designed for finger fractures. Often we did not immobilize the jaw, leaving the patient on a soft diet. For me the more severe the facial injury, the greater my enjoyment in repairing it. As I was on-call all of the time, if we went to the cinema I had to show the usherette where I was sitting so she could get me if needed. Any where else I called in leaving a telephone number. I loved the life, the job and the hospital. Only the pay was lousy.

Mining injuries from the Nottinghamshire coalfield as well as Road Traffic Accidents supplied the patients with several multiple facial fractures. The face was repaired rather like a jigsaw. Repair the orbits and cheekbones and fix them back onto the frontal bone or forehead. Repair the broken lower jaw to restore the dental arch and then reduce the middle part of the face until the dental occlusion of both jaws was correct. Some mid-face fractures were squashed and impacted whilst others were 'floaters'. Preoperatively, there was a time consuming process of taking impressions of sound teeth so that the dental technicians could produce cast silver cap splints in sections for multiple jaw fractures. These were cemented onto the teeth preoperatively if the patient's condition allowed, and used to reduce and fix the fractures together. The upper splints held a bar which projected out of the mouth which was attached to a frame on the forehead held in a plaster head cap. Steel wires were inserted through the cheek tissue and attached to the back of the upper splint and to the forehead frame in order to hold the mid facial bones firmly upwards. The jaws were fixed together in the correct anatomical position. When complete the patient who looked like a walking TV aerial existed on a fluid diet and had to sleep on their back without turning. I gained considerable pleasure from this work and seeing the final result after removing all fixations about a month later. We discharged the patient home about a week post-op together with their fixations.

Patients with multiple lacerations produced by contact from car windscreens were time consuming but also rewarding – unfortunately, one had to wait a year or two for the scars to soften before seeing the final result. Many of these patients presented with a mixture of extensive lacerations and small irregular cuts. The former were easy to explore and remove bits of glass or debris. The small cuts were the problem for each had to be probed to find and then remove the pieces of penetrating glass. In those days pressure upon operating theatres meant this work was done late at night as the non-life threatening cases were booked after acute surgical emergencies. This caused me much irritation and loss of sleep. Next morning, of course, there were clinics or booked operating lists as normal. My manual training and dexterity came to my assistance with this work and I rapidly became accepted in the A & E Department as the person to deal with facial lacerations.

By the end of that year we only referred burns and significant skin loss to the plastic surgeons. Tom did not do resections for malignancy over which the ENT and plastic surgeons disputed. The stupidity of all this competition was that every discipline was overwhelmed by work and had enormously long waiting lists.

Wyn Williams, the plastic surgeon, extracted retribution from me for this clinical experience. Years later I applied for a consultant job in Nottingham. Brian Hayes from Stoke-on-Trent, the external assessor and friend of the now deceased Tom, rang me the night before to tell the incumbent acting oral surgeon would get the job and Wyn Williams did not want anyone medically qualified appointed, particularly me, and that is what happened.

Because the anaesthetists were always busy elsewhere, I offered to give gaseous anaesthetics in the A & E Department for Colles fractures, nail removal and abscess drainage. Before long I was giving regular anaesthetics in Casualty. Senior staff nurses manipulated the wrist fractures and put on the plaster. Abscesses of breast and fingers were common, requiring drainage under GA. These huge abscesses are rarely seen in the UK today. Antibiotics and better hygiene have eliminated most of them. Nor would a dental house surgeon be allowed to give anaesthetics, or nurses manipulate fractures.

One Sunday afternoon I was walking from the wards back to the Mess when Sister called me from Casualty. The A&E doctor on call wasn't answering his lights (he was taking a bath) and a patient had just been brought in by ambulance with obstructed breathing. When I saw him, his respiration and heart beat were negligible and his mouth was full of pus. As I sucked it out I could see his throat was grossly swollen. I had never seen a tracheotomy performed but I had read how to do it so I did one. Still he did not breathe and his pulse was absent. I had not seen internal cardiac massage done either, but in the continued absence of a doctor, I opened his chest (external cardiac massage was not practised then). The rib spreader kept slipping and my fingers took a bashing. Despite everything, the heart remained unresponsive and the patient was declared dead. There was considerable fuss about all of this and the poor Casualty Officer got it in the neck for not being available. The hospital administrator demanded that my involvement would not be made public. I felt quite hurt at this but my clinical and nursing colleagues were very supportive of me.

8 Dental Fellowship and Oral Surgery Registrar, in Chertsey

Most junior doctors were single in those days and the Mess was our home. Despite working long hours, the Mess social life was tremendous. There was a dining room in which senior medical staff joined us for lunch with waitress service and we were well fed and cared for. Half of the 'burning money' (money given for signing cremation certificates) went into the Mess fund to pay for monthly dinners to which one or two consultants were invited. After a good meal, wine and a speech or two, the consultants departed and the gramophone came out for dancing. Nurses in civvies appeared as if by magic and an alcoholic orgy of dancing, fun and games commenced. These were splendid occasions. More than once I was called upon to repair somebody when I had had a few. One operating list on the morning following such a party was too much for me and Tom sent me to bed. He said it with a smile for we had established a special relationship by then.

My twelve months ended too quickly and I was to go to the residential course at the RCS to do a course for the Part 1 FDS. At the final Mess dinner, Graham Langdale, the Mess President, wished me well and threw a pewter tankard across the table as a presentation from the Mess. In my alcoholic state it came as a shock and I couldn't say thank you properly because of sobbing. Unexpected kindnesses can do that to me.

My year in Nottingham set me on a new career which satisfied my professional aspirations. I could not have had a better boss, friend, advisor or father figure than Tom. It was from him I got the habit of referring to people as Dear Boy or Dear Girl. His influence and his memories are with me still. Sadly, he died prematurely aged 53. Years before he had fallen off a horse damaging his neck. As his referred neck pain worsened, it was decided to fuse his cervical spine for which he was admitted into the Robert Jones and Agnes Hunt Orthopaedic Hospital, Oswestry. All went well post-operatively until he developed hepatitis. In a delirium he fell out of his plaster bed onto the floor, resulting in his bone grafts extruding through the wound on the back of his neck. The neck wound healed by granulation with deep scarring and his nerve root pains worsened. Despite this he remained cheerful in public but increasingly required more and more alcohol and analgesia to get to sleep. One night he took too much of both and did not wake up. The Inquest verdict was accidental death. His death left me bereft. I was then a medical student and knew I had lost a dear friend, a supporter and advisor. He was fun and had class. He, more than any other of my clinical teachers, left his mark upon me.

Still having my Rhodesia earned money in the bank I could afford to enrol on the primary FDS residential course at the Nuffield College of the RCS, London. Post graduate NHS financial support and study leave in the late 50s was a concept, not a reality. It was the first casualty of a financial crisis as the hospital management could not see an immediate financial or clinical return for their investment. Primary Fellowship exams demanded a high knowledge base and the pass rate was relatively low at 30-40%. It was common to require several attempts at the exam. Bearing in mind my inherent laziness, it seemed wise to lock myself up for the six or eight weeks of graft. It was a good course with quality lecturers who made the anatomy, physiology, pathology and associated subjects plausible, even enjoyable. Professor Jack Last believed in the use of mnemonics to remember anatomy, e.g. 'Lazy French tarts sit naked in anticipation' for the nerves of the superior orbital fissure and 'As she lay naked Oswald's penis slowly mounted' for the branches of the external carotid artery. I used these and others to teach dental students later on. How dull life must be in these days of political correctness.

Norman Rowe

The College accommodation was excellent, the food more than adequate and there were formal dinners with College worthies and parties around Christmas time, as a result of which there usually was a tap on my door about 5.30pm. I am certain this member of staff was a very important factor in my passing the exam at the first attempt. At the concluding lecture on physiology, Dr. Perrit, an extravert and successful teacher, threw down the gauntlet, asking us to question him on anything 'Why do we sneeze when we get a draught on our body?' I asked. He ignored me. I still don't know why a shiver and a sneeze go together.

During the course I applied for the registrar post associated with N.L. Rowe, fast becoming established as one of the most successful oral surgeons in the country. His main base was at Queen Mary's Hospital, Roehampton, but there was a registrar to cover the rest of the area of the South West Metropolitan Hospital Board based at St. Peter's Hospital, Chertsey, with operating lists and outpatient clinics in Hazelmere with outpatients' clinics in Aldershot General, Woking General and St. Richards, Chichester. Norman, medically and dentally qualified, had passed his FDS, RCS along with Tom. I believe Tom had rung Norman which must have assisted me. The interview started badly for me. His first question to me was, 'What about this stupid letter about a medical qualification?' I had written to the BDJ attacking the requirement of both a medical and dental qualification for a second consultant with Norman Rowe. I didn't know I would be seeking a job with him when I wrote it, and included the phrase the 'rubber stamp of the double qualification'. It was a measure of Norman or the quality of the other candidates that I was appointed.

St. Peter's Hospital had been built to care for American casualties in World War 2. It was a collection of concrete single storey huts. My memory suggests the wards had ridged roofs of asbestos sheeting but the nearby accommodation for nurses and doctors had flat roofs. The nurses' home accommodation blocks were next to the Doctors' Mess which had a small bar in which a party could start in a flash. The junior medical staff were recruited either from St. Thomas', the 'starboard watch', whilst the 'port watch' were from St. George's plus a few like me. The starboard watch was on-call one week and port watch the next. The Casualty Unit took in major trauma, including facial injuries, and it was not long before I had cornered the facial lacerations as well as the toothaches. Covering an area from Surrey to Sussex produced a substantial mileage and I found my expenses sufficient to pay for petrol and contribute to a new car. I bought a new TR3A sports car on HP and had seat belts fitted. Driving down to Hazelmere or Chichester on a summer's day on the A3 with the hood down was fun.

'Cold' lists were booked for St. Peter's where our beds were in two wards. Facial trauma patients were admitted to any ward with a bed available. Success in getting such beds seemed to depend upon the relationships established with the Ward Sister or Senior Staff Nurse at Mess parties. In Hazlemere, we worked in the Holy Cross Hospital, run and staffed by a Catholic order of nuns. The hospital originally had cared for patients with tuberculosis but as these had become fewer they had accepted NHS work. It was a very happy hospital to work in with quality lunches, usually shared with Father Caffrey the local priest, who unusually wore a very obvious toupee. One summer day he requested a lift up to Hindhead. The hood was down and I determined to show off the 2 litre engine's power. There was a sudden call of alarm and I saw Caffrey grab his head, whilst in the driver's mirror, I saw his toupee fly away. It took us ages to find it, perhaps increased by the tears in my eyes caused by laughter. The Father was searching for evidence of miracles at that time for the canonisation of a local would-be Saint. I said it would be a miracle if we found his wig; Father Caffrey never forgave me.

The ward nursing skills of the nuns varied considerably. None of them were State Registered Nurses. Several nuns were obviously embarrassed by our male presence and seemed most introverted (they all came from

Southern Ireland), and were subject to the Mother Superior who was straight laced and very superior. However, we struck gold in Sister Jarlath, the senior theatre sister, who was not only competent but was full of fun and a joy to work with. She laughed, played tricks upon you and enjoyed life in a very un-nun like manner. She usually participated in the showering of junior male staff who were leaving. She would assist us with the pushing of the unfortunate individual, still in his theatre suit, into the shower, usually running with cold water. On one occasion, hearing the hullabaloo, the Mother Superior came into the changing room to see a soaked Sister Jarlath fully involved. I don't remember her punishment but I am sure it involved a lot of 'Hail Marys'. Clearly she yearned for more from life and fell in love with my successor, an Asian doctor, and left the Order to live with him. Alas she did not enjoy her new life for long, for she developed a virulent carcinoma of the breast and succumbed at an early age. I expect there were some who saw this as a just punishment but I hope that she had some happiness and contentment before she died. Jarlath was never meant to be incarcerated, playing the children's games that I watched her colleagues do on the lawn on summer afternoons. I felt a deep sorrow for them. Their lives seemed unfulfilled and subjugated. To my surprise, Jarlath confirmed that they too used the cords from around their waists to flagellate their backs as I had seen alleged on a TV programme.

Work wise, the Holy Cross was a great success. In addition to assisting a consultant list I had my own operating list, working with an Austrian Jewish refugee, Consultant Anaesthetist Dr. Hans Kallenberg. He was a splendid person, a multi-talented linguist, music lover who also loved cricket. When a Test Match was being played we put a TV on the air conditioner in theatre whilst we operated. He would anaesthetise the next patient as I finished the one on the table, something now regarded as dangerous. Our work rate was enormous. Then my lists were limited to oral surgery, removing cysts, closing oro-antral fistulae, removing impacted wisdom and other teeth. There were regular excisions of areas of exuberant intra oral soft tissue produced by the wearing of over-extended dentures and I became skilled in taking skin grafts from the leg to cover the oral defect.

After about four months Ian Heslop took up his consultant post and matters became more organised and better behaved. We did our first two stage mandibular reduction. This involved an enormous, time consuming and essentially unnecessary preoperative work-up with planning down to the last millimetre. A lower tooth, usually a molar, was extracted from each side and the alveolar bone removed to expose the inferior neurovascular canal. A mucosal flap was rotated over the gap and sewn into place. After a month, under another general anaesthetic, the lower border of the jaw was exposed through a neck incision and the inferior bone removed to expose the nerve bundle from below. The anterior jaw was then moved posteriorly when silver cap splints were connected together with all the teeth in correct occlusion. The osteotomy usually healed without much problem in six weeks.

Happily, this expensive and time consuming technique would soon be replaced by simpler, more effective methods. Then we were sailing in uncharted waters, believing that an elective osteotomy should never be exposed to the oral cavity in case infection resulted. Then only mandibular reduction procedures existed; this must have resulted in some patients having a normally sized lower jaw reduced instead of the upper jaw being brought forward. Another 'chinless wonder'. These were pioneering days. Norman Rowe was a stickler for detail and nothing was allowed to go wrong, for the plastic surgeons would have created mayhem which is probably why these cases were done in Hazlemere instead of Roehampton. It was all very exciting for me.

Life in the Mess at St. Peter's was fun. Few of us were married for then the life of a junior doctor was peripatetic. Essentially, the Mess was our home. Our dining room also provided lunch for consultants and there was, of course, maid service, the maids being Spanish. The manager of the Mess, Lady Blake, was the widow of a knight. She had a sense of humour for she was clearly surprised by our behaviour when off duty. When our furniture was replaced, without warning, one staff member found a neat pile of used condoms, that had been in his bedside cupboard, on his new bed . Because the Mess was a long building with rooms off a central corridor it was relatively easy to hear shrieks of pleasure from one or two noisy girlfriends as we sat in the bar having a nightcap. Such events assisted team building, but it was wiser to achieve silence if one wished to avoid the leg pulling afterwards.

There was a friendly competitiveness between the watches. The George's people believed you could always tell a Tommy's graduate but you couldn't tell him much. This competitiveness featured on the tennis courts and croquet lawn. I teamed up with John Stubbs, a compulsive cutting general surgeon and smoker, to play croquet. He had done his National Service and already had a PhD in Physiology. He was not good at exams and had trouble with the primary Fellowship, usually failing his physiology! Croquet can be cruel and the two of us became a useful pair being very unpleasant to our opponents. There was a small gap between the lawn and the pavement edging. I once knocked an opponent's ball too hard; it ran along this gap catching fire from the friction. We were impressed.

The late 1950s were the days of motor cycle clubs, and summer weekends were likely to provide a crop of injuries. It was not unusual for all of us to be involved with the various injuries. I was impressed by one who had several compound fractures of his forehead which had exposed his frontal lobes. One of his pupils was fixed, non reactive to light. Noel Pizey, a Thomas's senior registrar in Urology, said 'He's had it; you don't recover from a fixed pupil.' It turned out to be a glass eye. To be fair the patient's face was covered in blood and dirt. Poor Noel gained a nickname for which he never forgave us. I believe the patient recovered to a degree in the Atkinson Morley Hospital.

Impromptu Mess parties with such close proximity to nursing quarters could have a variety of consequences. Late one night we were in the bar having a nightcap (which was followed by a few more) when some wag suggested raiding the nurses' quarters. One of us was very small in stature and we crept into the nurses' quarters entering the bathroom and toilets. From the bathrooms we took numerous pants and bras from drying rails whilst the toilet doors were locked from the inside by our small colleague who then escaped through the window. We took the underwear to the flag pole outside the Administration building and after tying it onto the pole rope pulled it up to full flying glory. Plaster of Paris bandage was wound round the base of the pole, and rope completed the exercise. Next morning a large number of nurses were seen in their dressing gowns going to the main hospital for a pee. There was hell to play from the physicians' superintendent – a Tommy's man. We were ordered to buy replacement underwear and each person involved put £5 into the kitty – a goodly sum then. All ended well, however, when we had another party and invited guests willingly came to show off their new garments.

Not all parties ended so happily. One day I went to the orthopaedic ward to see a patient and was taken aside by a nurse who told me she was overdue. As our acquaintance was at best casual, this was a big shock and I had no recollection of anything untoward. Sister made it very clear she saw it as my problem and it certainly was even though I doubted that I was the cause. After a couple of days of torture, I summoned up courage to speak to one of the consultant gynaecologists at lunchtime and explained our/my predicament. I had picked the guy with the most outgoing personality and he said simply 'tell her to get in touch'. She had a D & C a few days later. I never thanked my senior colleague afterwards, believing that if I did it would throw doubt upon my denial. This was another mistake to add to the several regrets that have gradually accumulated. Of course, it is impossible to keep things like this a secret and my two bosses soon knew about it. Neither they nor their wives were impressed. Ian's wife said that I shouldn't be allowed to get away with it!

Receiving my FDSRCS diploma from Sir Arthur Porritt. Norman Rowe is in the background

It was clear I was in bad books. I worried about my future references.

My two years were drawing to a close. After reading the books and journals in my spare time, I entered the final Fellowship exam and to my surprise and delight passed it. In retrospect, I think the examiners knew little about modern oral surgery or maxillofacial surgery, but there it was; I had passed and have a photograph of my Diploma being presented by the Olympian and President, Sir Arthur Porritt. It had become apparent my discipline was on the move and if I were to be appointed to a good job, I would benefit by being medically qualified. I also was offended by being called a 'bloody dentist' by the medical housemen I was teaching to sew up wounds. I was still single and knew I wanted to know more medicine, so I decided it was now or never for me to go to medical school. I was 29 when I was accepted by Newcastle and the Royal Free in London. I chose London where I believed it would be easier to find dental work to cover my expenses.

9 Back to School as a Medical Student

I remain deeply grateful to the Royal Free Medical School and Hospital for enabling me to get a medical qualification and to get on the medical register, which made it possible for me to have a varied, interesting, enjoyable and successful consultant career. I entered medical school aged 29, about 10 years older than the majority of the year, and left it at age 32.

We had eight months to complete the preclinical subjects for the 2nd MB exam. Much of the anatomy, physiology and associated studies I had already covered twice before. The three years residency and work in general hospitals put my learning into a clinical context which made it much easier to remember. I switched from the MB Course to do the Conjoint Qualification, with permission from the medical school, and I managed to obtain a reduction in the period of clinical training, because of my previous experience, from the Royal Colleges of Physicians and Surgeons.

The Royal Free Hospital Medical School in Hunter Street had originally been exclusively for women. Government subsidy and early equal opportunities were breaking down this exclusivity in all universities and the Free took a minority of male students. In the year I entered, there were seven out of the seventy four. Four of us were dental graduates with Sandy Young, like me, having been a registrar in oral surgery. My admission interview was by the Dean, Dr. Frances Gardner, a physician of note who later married the swash-buckling chest surgeon George Qvist on the staff of the Free. We were admitted into the third year which meant we could not waste time at the 2nd MB exam which completed the academic year. Maturity made academic work much easier, particularly as much of it was familiar to us. In anatomy Sandy Young, myself and another dentist, Arnold Miles, who later became a chest physician in the USA, worked together on our cadaver. Already having surgical skills, anatomical dissection was easy and we whizzed through it. Biochemistry caused me my usual problems, but all were passed.

The Royal Free Hospital in Gray's Inn Road had originally been a cavalry barracks, complete with stables. Large Nightingale wards were the norm. Obstetric experience was gained in the Liverpool Road Hospital in Islington, among a largely Greek Cypriot community, whilst Hampstead General Hospital was an outpost of surgical clinical teaching and a reminder that London could be very pleasant. I was exposed to female consultants as clinical teachers for the first time and several gained my respect. There were others, however, who verbally abused the female students, particularly one Dr. Una Ledingham, who reduced some girls to tears. Our weakness was made obvious by the short white jackets or 'bum freezers' worn by the students. I felt humiliated by these jackets, yet on more than one occasion, patients thought I was the doctor and not the much younger registrar who wore a long white coat.

Once I watched a registrar do a sternal puncture causing considerable pain to the patient; I told him quietly he should learn how to give local analgesia painlessly and give it time to work before ramming in the trephine. He became very superior until I told him I had given more local injections than he had had hot dinners. Another nonsense we had to tolerate was the ritual we went through to greet and say a farewell to Dr. Hancock. He was a visiting physician, who would drive his Rolls into the courtyard to be met by his staff and students drawn up in a line. We would then follow 'our lord' to the ward to do his teaching rounds which were actually very good. He was also a very nice man. There remained the God-like aura of consultants and having many respectful girls in the Free meant retaining more of it than was good for anyone. Some consultants took advantage of the young ladies.

Quite often, in good summer weather, I would walk from the Free back to Harley Street where I now lived. However, the winters in London in the early 60s were bad and worsened by smog. This and tobacco smoke could be so bad that it was not easy to see detail from one end of the ward to the other. One dark night, I left the Free to find the deep smog had caused all traffic, even buses, to stop so I set off to walk home. The acrid smoke made breathing unpleasant. I got to the end of Gray's Inn Road near Kings Cross and started to cross the road to go up to Holborn. Halfway across I was lost. I continued walking, scared I could be run over. I did not meet any one or any vehicle but at last came to the roadside. However, I could not determine where I was but continued walking. Street names were invisible until I found that I was in Islington having done a 'U' turn. I must have been able to get home somehow but the memory of my helplessness and the awfulness of smog remains. I thought about this several times when caught in sea fog in my boat off the Pembrokeshire Coast years later. I always took compass bearings if fog was about so I could get back to my mooring. Boating or flying without instruments can be an unpleasant experience.

Initially, I shared a flat with a fellow dental graduate, Julian Layton, who was a medical student at University College Hospital, at 140 Harley Street, a good address for an undergraduate. The fourth floor apartment was notable for the several trainee orthoptists who lived above us and the Gynaecologist who had rooms below. We used to read the referral letters left outside his door at night by his secretary for him to read in the morning. They all read 'Please see Miss So and So who suffers from primary amenorrhoea and a state of anxiety.' So much for patient confidentiality and the illegality of abortion for the well off.

The apartment worked well even though there was only one bedroom with two single beds. We were both broad minded and flexible. Julian came back one day to tell me he had just met a nurse at UCH he was going to marry which he did later. We had a party one evening to which I invited some medical student colleagues from the Free. One of the girls was attractive in a white coat but when she arrived in a figure revealing dress, an electric shock hit me in the stomach and spread all over me. It was the only time in my life that I experienced coup de foudre. Much later she told me that she had had a bet with her friends that she would go out with me. This she did and more and we were engaged within a year or so.

I parked my TR3 in Regents Park outer circular road, using it as required or at weekends. One day I found my car had gone. I got it back about two weeks later covered in finger print powder. It had a damaged wing. It had been used in a bank robbery and had had its engine tuned!

With Julian about to get married I had to find alternative accommodation. Through my old St. Peter's contacts I heard that some of their friends were looking for people to share a terminal lease of 100 Walton Street, SW3, just off Kensington High Street between Chelsea and South Kensington. What a place to live! It was a terraced house owned by Cadogan Estates and due for demolition. Directly opposite was a pub, Buckingham Palace was around the corner and Harrods down the road. As Sloane Square was a stone's throw away, we were in the centre of the Universe. The house inhabitants consisted of Mike Hunter, an orthopaedic registrar, Nim Ellam of Ellams Duplicators, John Fanstone, in advertising, John Howard, a trainee Ophthalmologist and me. We developed a way of living together, partying together and having a very enjoyable time in that house. Initially, the landlord opposite thought we were a group of homosexuals but as our lounge was on the first floor and contained a double sofa bed which was used as required, he soon realised he had made a mistake.

We had a rota for cooking and our shared housekeeping costs included a cleaner. The only minor repetitive problem for me was Mike's dislike of me boiling my underpants and handkerchiefs in a saucepan to maintain their pristine whiteness. I found the enormous quantities of butter and marmalade he put on his toast unacceptable so we called it a draw. We got on famously, along with our girlfriends, making a big happy family. Girlfriends became fiancées, exams were passed, life was good. It is a considerable sadness this good start did not continue through life for us all.

Mike married Inga, who came from a very rich Danish family. In due course he became an orthopaedic consultant in Basingstoke where nearby they had a beautiful house and two sons – one alas with severe cerebral palsy. Mike died in his early 50s from carcinoma of the kidney. I went to say my farewells to him and we walked together in his garden for this surreal purpose. His funeral was an emotional time for all of us from the house. Nim married Julia, a beautiful if scatter-brained daughter of a rich Sussex farmer. They too had two children. Although Ellams Duplicators folded, they had plenty of cash and lived in a beautiful thatched house in Dorset. Julia died in her 40s from a malignant cerebral tumour and Nim died in his early 60s from lung cancer, still smoking cigarettes to the very end. It was another depressing experience to drive down to say goodbye to him. John Fanstone had two severe strokes in his early 40s which left him with impaired speech and motor function and unable to work. His wife and family lovingly cared for him until his death. John married Paddy and they thrived but without children.

10 Part Time Dental Practice and a Brush with the General Dental Council

While I was a Medical Student I covered my daily expenses by finding part time work, paid by commission, in a dental practice in Kingsbury. I worked Wednesday afternoons, Friday evenings and alternate Saturdays all day; this enabled me to pay my way. Happily, my medical studies were paid for by a student grant from my old local authority in Sunderland. The dental practice was owned by a dentist who did the paperwork whilst employing several people to do the clinical work. It suited me well but I was I knackered by the time I went home at night, usually having fish and chips on the way back. I earned enough to run my car, go on holiday and pay my way in the house.

One day, a female patient requested that I provide her with a skeletal metal denture privately. As she did not seem flush with money I suggested that I could get her some NHS money to assist towards the cost. I submitted an EC18 form, seeking approval to do this. I completed some NHS dental work to make her dentally fit, and filled in the EC17 form and fortunately writing on the back that the denture had been provided outside the NHS. The EC18 form was returned from the Estimates Board but agreeing a small NHS sum for the denture. I rang up the boss, Alan Seymour, who was upstairs and told him what I had done to help the patient but that there appeared to be confusion about the provision of the private denture. He told me to get it finished and leave all the paperwork to him. This I did and then I forgot all about it.

About a year later, Seymour told me that I owed him £200 for he had been fined that amount by the Middlesex Executive Council for mixing private practice with NHS work. Initially I had difficulty in remembering the matter but when I did I declined to pay up. As we were both members, Seymour agreed to the Medical Protection Society arbitrating between us. We met the Dental Secretary who decided I should pay Seymour 30% of £200 for misusing an EC18 but he was at fault for signing and sending up the forms. Seymour denied all knowledge of my asking his advice but accepted the result of arbitration.

Months later, just before I was to sit my surgical finals, I received notification that the General Dental Council (GDC) was to enquire whether I should be struck off the Dentists' Register for illegal practices! I was absolutely shattered and immediately sought the support of the Medical Protection Society. It turned out that Seymour had consistently denied all knowledge of the matter to the Middlesex Executive Council, blaming it all upon his assistant. I was already aware that his senior nurse, who I had consulted at the time and who suggested that I rang Seymour, also denied all knowledge of the event. Apart from my own writing on the EC17 that the denture was provided outside of the NHS there was no other supportive evidence. My case would involve proving two people were lying. The GDC hearing occurred a week or so before my surgical examination. My barrister, provided by the Protection Society, seemed unsympathetic and gave me strict instructions on how to answer questions. The prosecution case was damning and the first my poor mother knew of it were the headlines in the Sunderland Echo. I had not told her of my troubles; we were both unhappy.

When I was called into the witness stand I admitted, on oath, that I had inadvertently misused the form in the mistaken belief it could produce a contribution towards the cost of private treatment. I confirmed it was my writing on the back of the EC17 and that I had not attempted to hide what I had done. I stressed that, not knowing what to do, I had sought clarification from Seymour and did as he advised. I repeated that I only filled in the form to assist the patient, not myself. Seymour went into the box the next morning. He denied all knowledge of my seeking his advice and had not seen that I had misused the one form. It all looked very unpleasant for me. Quite unexpectedly for me, the GDC barrister after gaining further confirmation from Seymour that he had not been consulted by me, presented him with a letter written by him to the Dental Estimates Board explaining that his assistant had used the EC17 by mistake and that the denture was provided by a separate private arrangement. 'How if you know nothing about this could you have written this letter?' Suddenly, the spotlight on me went off and onto Seymour. The Barrister started to give Seymour a hard time but was stopped by the Chairman, Sir Robert Bradlaw, my old Dean at Newcastle, who pointed out that Seymour was not being investigated.

The case collapsed and shortly afterwards the Chairman announced there was no case for my name to be erased from the Register and I was free to go. I burst into tears; such was my intense relief. As I waited outside for my Counsel, one of the Tribunal members, Professor MacGregor from Birmingham, came up and shook my hand and said surprisingly, 'Sorry – we got the wrong person.' My mother was delighted when I told her the result and she attempted, unsuccessfully, to get the Echo to print the result with the same size headlines as they gave the prosecution. I requested the Medical Protection Society to sue the General Dental Council for putting me through misery when they had in their possession the very evidence which destroyed their own case but they refused to do so.

My surgical finals followed soon after. In the Examination Halls at Queen's Square, the first paper was a multiple choice and I finished it quickly. I then noted several people around had pulled out cribs from pockets. One, an African, sat next to me. I told him that if he did not put it away I would call the invigilator. He did so. After I left the hall I called at the office and told them I had just left the examination room where several people were cheating in the back of the hall. I learned subsequently several invigilators suddenly entered the room.

My viva went well. I deliberately wore my Royal College of Surgeons tie which caught the examiner's eye. He wanted to know how I could wear the tie before joining the College? The viva was nearly over before I had finished my explanation. Shortly afterwards I heard my named called amongst those new members of the College and we proceeded to take the College oath. I did not see the African examinee amongst us.

Not long afterwards I received a reminder to pay my registration fee to the GDC. I replied that as they had tried so hard to throw me off I would not bother to stay on. Happily, Medical Registration would cover my requirements. I never forgave the GDC or re-registered with them. As far as I was concerned I had a dental qualification and some very useful knowledge but from now on my allegiance was to Medicine. My experience before and during the hearing, knowing that my career was serious threatened, was the worst of my life. I did not even wish to acknowledge that I was in a dental specialty later on. I was pleased by the European Union which required the dual qualification of Medicine and Dentistry for the medical mono-speciality maxillofacial surgery. I passed my Obstetrics & Gynaecology finals without too much difficulty, although I got a shock in my clinical viva when I did not realise the patient under the cover was 5ft tall and her husband a giant. I did not see her standing and adrenaline misled my powers of observation. I cannot remember my medical finals but they were the last exams I sat. I qualified LRCP MRCS.

Thirteen years had flashed by since I had embarked upon my undergraduate dental course. What had I gained? I had come to terms with my inherent laziness and the realisation that I had to work if I was to achieve anything. I had probably joined the wrong profession but my transfer to hospital practice had satisfied my career aspiration even at the cost of gaining another qualification. Dental practice had increased my manual dexterity and patient management. To work on apprehensive, ungrateful patients required special skills. I had seen and smelt Africa which carried me through the indignities of being a medical student. Having now learned some basic medicine and surgery, I was ready to embark upon the last phase of my training to be a consultant.

11 House Physician Croydon, House Surgeon Wandsworth

I had a pre-registration year to complete before I could contemplate going back to oral surgery. I did a week's locum in general practice and I got a couple of weeks in Harold Wood Hospital, Essex in general medicine before I started as a house physician in the Mayday Hospital, Croydon, working for Dr. Stanley Baker, a bachelor and very sound general physician who drove an Austin Westminster then – the poor man's Rolls Royce and lived with his mother. If he was not homosexual, he was asexual and seemed embarrassed by female flesh. In those days we followed in the old surgical saying – 'If you don't put your fingers in, you put your foot in it.' A rectal examination known as a 'PR' was an essential part of the examination for any abdominal problem. Now and again on the ward round the registrar or I judged it necessary for Dr. Baker to do one on a female. He would avoid doing so like the plague but when he had to, the patient would have her backside on the bedside with Sister standing holding her hand whilst covering all the flesh she could. Baker would go down on his knees, as if in prayer, and with his eyes averted or shut, gingerly stick his finger (in a lubricated latex finger cott) around the anus until he finally made it into the rectum. If the target was large he could find it quickly but his distaste and his kneeling position stopped him from penetrating all of the angles necessary to examine the pelvis. We, his juniors, shook silently with laughter. We had two large single sex wards of over 60 patients which were always full.

There are several things I remember about my time at the Mayday – an old building with open Nightingale wards, long overdue for demolition. A new reception area was constructed to transfer patients from the ambulances onto hospital trolleys. On its opening, the trolley was pushed round the corner towards the main building, only to jam because the angle of the corridor was too tight. The patient had to be lifted by two porters round the corner onto another trolley. Such incompetence did nothing to commend the planners to the doctors.

There were several surprises for me on the medical wards at the Mayday. On the female ward almost all of the patients were constipated. I carried out a detailed review of their fluid intakes and nearly all were seriously deficient; with the Sister's support, we pushed fluids in all forms at these ladies. They complained furiously, some about drowning on land. I left before any obvious result was apparent but did learn that ladies do not like bed pans. I was delighted to read that this topic resurfaced in medical circles in the year 2008.

After I certified the death of a male patient, I had a call from a solicitor who told me the patient had left £50 for a doctor to cut his wrists before cremation to confirm his death. £50 was a lot of money to me. I rang the undertaker to arrange a suitable time to do this but he said he had already embalmed him. I told him he was a crook for embalming a corpse for only 24 hours. I rang the solicitor and said it was not worth carrying out the task. He agreed. I was a fool, I should have done what the patient wanted and taken the money.

One day I was called to see a girl in her late teens or early twenties who had taken an overdose of either Aspirin or Paracetamol. She was semi-conscious and became very ill with multiple organ failure. Everybody who looked after her worked hard. She survived and slowly recovered over a period of several weeks. She was discharged to a psychiatric hospital.

Towards the end of my six months of general medicine I was called to Admissions to find the same patient. She had been discharged home from the psychiatric hospital the previous day and that night had swallowed all of her take-home drugs. Whether it was tiredness or anger I'm not sure but I remember thinking, 'She is so bloody useless she can't even kill herself'. I'm not proud of this but some patients can try one's patience; obviously I was not temperamentally suitable to be a psychiatrist. I left before she was discharged.

I did not apply for jobs in teaching hospitals with their wall to wall carpeting of registrars; I wanted actual clinical practice. Towards the end of my six months in Croydon, I was lucky to read the advertisement for house surgeons at the Bolingbroke Hospital, Wandsworth Common. It seemed too good to be true. Responsible to four teaching hospital consultants, the work covered general surgery, urology, gynaecology with night time and weekend casualty cover and occasional ENT and ophthalmology. These were the days when no thought was given to what was a reasonable workload for junior doctors, but for me the breadth of clinical exposure was ideal. I learned later that I nearly did not get the job for there was doubt that the Resident Surgical Officer could control me! Ageism already existed. The RSO, a surgical registrar, was R.J. Heald, known as Bill. This was another bonus for he turned out to be someone upon whom the Gods had smiled. Good looking and charming, he had left Cambridge with a 1st in Natural Sciences to complete his clinical studies at Guy's. His intelligence was obvious and he was a natural cutter, with his skills widening with the several disciplines we covered. Bill was content for me to operate on my own once he or the consultants were convinced I was a safe pair of hands. This resulted in my being able to do the lumps and bumps, appendicectomy, varicose veins and a few hernias. This hands-on experience far exceeded what I would have had at the Free or from the usual house job, and assisting the consultants at table taught me much useful technique for my subsequent career.

Peter Phillips, a Charing Cross urologist, was a delight to work for, apart from his habit of turning up to do a ward round shortly after I had got to bed. Radical prostatectomy, which was the usual treatment for prostate cancer, was pretty unpleasant for everybody. One of my Saturday tasks was the boogie clinic where a number of elderly men had their urethral strictures, the result of gonorrhoea caught in the First World War, dilated. It was a clinic of considerable humour – they were proud of their war wound and long used to the procedure and being exposed to the nurses.

There were two general surgeons, one of whom was J.M. Pullen from St. Thomas's. He rarely turned up for his operating lists or clinics, leaving them to Bill. He turned up, however, for on-spec ward rounds to check on what was being done in his name. He used to upset Bill by saying 'Hoppy, come with me.' I would leave Bill operating to take him around the wards. He spent most of his time in Harley Street and had two Rolls Royces – one given by an Arab prince. Rex Lawrie from Guy's was quite different. A specialist paediatric surgeon, he was an excellent clinical and general surgeon. He was also a good teacher with a pleasing urbane personality who fully fulfilled his NHS responsibilities. During the war he had served in a facial injury unit which gave us a head start. George Pinker was the Queen's accoucheur. He too was a pleasure to work for, though there were only gynaecology beds and clinics in the hospital.

George Pinker had an outpatient clinic at the Bolingbroke. I did not look forward to these for the patients came in with their stockings rolled down around their ankles and somehow I never became entirely comfortable looking at vaginas in cold blood. In due course I became used to them and even the odd patient who uttered sighs of pleasure as they were examined. George would occasionally see patients who wished to avoid medical students at St. Mary's but could not afford to go privately. I had to take the history from a couple complaining of infertility. He was a Cambridge Don. 'How often do you have intercourse?' I asked. 'Three times a year, Christmas, Easter and on summer holidays.' 'I believe Mr. Pinker will suggest repetition as a trial treatment,' I replied. He was genuinely surprised.

Alternate Saturday mornings were set aside for the house surgeon to do a D & C list of young women who we admitted on Friday evening with inevitable abortions. We believed that we knew the abortionist who came riding onto the Common on a moped bicycle every Friday. When I suggested to George Pinker we should shop him to the police, he did not agree as this way girls were evacuated in safe, sterile circumstances rather than in dirty backrooms and it was best left alone. Every alternate Saturday morning I operated upon about 8-12 girls. One Friday evening a young Scots girl was admitted. When I went to examine her I found her in labour. Before long she delivered a baby somewhere about 9 inches long. I looked at this moving, jerking object in amazement. 'What the hell do we do now?' I asked the Staff Nurse. 'I don't know,' she replied. I said, 'Put this in the ward cupboard,' as I put this human object in a kidney bowl and covered it up. We waited for the placenta but nothing happened. Her pains started again and my exploring finger felt another head emerging. Before long another perfectly formed, but hopelessly premature infant was put in a kidney dish and taken to the same cupboard where it could expire with its sibling. The patient had come down to London from Glasgow because she could not tell her parents about her situation and had an abortion procedure. No one had briefed me or the Staff Nurse on what to do in such a situation and I was quite disturbed by the episode. I made the obvious comparison between my experience in Wandsworth and the referral letters I used to read in Harley Street – 'Please see Miss..... who has primary amenorrhoea and a state of anxiety.'

There was a significant immigrant West Indian population in the area. George Pinker, later Sir George, gave me some early useful advice. 'If a West Indian lady comes in bleeding per vagina, work on the likelihood of fibroids or an inevitable abortion. You won't go far wrong.' One evening at about 9.00 pm I was called to see such a patient who was bleeding copiously. She was enormous which added to the difficulty of finding her pulse. Her skin was pallid and sweaty. Her pulse was weak and her blood pressure barely recordable. This was not bleeding from fibroids. She was sufficiently conscious to tell me her period was two months late. The probability of an ectopic pregnancy was paramount in my mind as I sent nurses to call the resident surgical officer by telephone from a dinner at nearby Guy's and the on-call theatre team. The hospital porter was sent for four units of O+ blood from the blood bank.

As I was attempting to find a vein in which to insert a catheter the news came back that Bill was returning post haste but the theatre team was working already on an emergency at our sister hospital at Putney. Because of her obesity and low blood pressure I could not find a vein so I did three separate cut downs – one on each lower arm and one on her shin to expose veins into which it was very easy to insert the cannula through which we could push in fluid. By the time Bill arrived in his best suit three saline drips were running quickly. I told Bill the principal findings and the bad news about the theatre team which, of course, included our anaesthetist on-call. Bill looked at the blood loss and the patient who was slipping in and out of consciousness. 'Hoppy – you will give the anaesthetic,' he said. It never occurred to me to say no – my previous experience of giving anaesthetics and working with anaesthetists for years gave me enough confidence to agree. I realised that I could not, dare not, induce with intra venous agents for we had no idea of her weight and I had no experience of giving Pentothal.

Somehow we got the patient onto the trolley. Her body hung over both its sides. The porter had not yet returned from the Blood Bank so Bill and I pushed the trolley towards the lift. I was at the head and I kept my fingers on her neck pulse. As we entered the lift I suddenly became aware I could not feel a pulse. 'Bill,' I said, 'It's too late, she's gone'. The upper half of this huge body raised itself, 'No boss, ay's not gone yet!' Bloody hell, I thought. We got to the theatre floor and into theatre. Bill and I lifted her with the canvas and wooden poles onto the operating table and I remember well her abdominal flesh hanging over each side. Bill brought in the boxes of sterilised theatre instruments whilst I pulled the anaesthetic machine into position. I turned on the nitrous oxide, oxygen and Trilene and put the face mask on the patient. Bill left the theatre but soon returned having taken off his jacket and put on his mask, gown and gloves. He set out the instruments and waited for me to give the OK. Within a few minutes her breathing settled, her eyelids were unresponsive and her arm floppy. 'OK Bill – go ahead.'

The abdomen was opened in a flash and the pints of free blood sucked out. It did not take long to find which Fallopian tube was bleeding and clip it off. 'We've done it,' said Bill.

Unfortunately, within a few seconds the patient started to move – even to attempt to get up. I turned every anaesthetic knob up full and put my weight on her shoulders to hold her down. Bill was pushing down hard inside her abdomen! 'For God's sake, Hoppy, get her to sleep.' It was now clear that she had been unconscious from blood loss and not anaesthesia. Gradually peace returned and Bill was able to finish off and close the abdomen. By this time the blood had arrived and we pushed it in. Early next morning George Pinker arrived and we took him to see our patient. She was sitting up having her breakfast without any memory of the previous night.

Today, emergency treatment is concentrated in special units and ambulance crews are aware of where to take patients with specific problems. Patients taken ill can present at a non-scheduled hospital; today I doubt if this lady would survive even if she did.

Junior doctors today do very little operating before they become Specialist registrars. Because of shifts and the European Working Time Directive, it now requires three doctors to do the work of one. Today their clinical exposure and experience is drastically reduced. Training posts with in-depth experience of several disciplines are non-existent. Our West Indian lady owes her life to Bill's surgical ability gained from operating from his surgical jobs. No house surgeon today would have sufficient experience to ever contemplate giving an anaesthetic and would certainly be frightened off by Health and Safety and General Medical Council regulations. As a result of the Labour Government's desire to increase the number of consultants and to appoint them at an earlier age, we will soon have consultants who have a limited clinical field. It will require a committee of them to arrive at a diagnosis. They will be specialists not consultants. Our lucky West Indian patient should be glad she had her ectopic in the bad old days.

The workload derived from four consultants was enormous and I was fully stretched. Our visiting ophthalmologist was a large and aggressive female I did not like. Her occasional lists were a nuisance for I never had the time or the inclination to clerk in her patients. She complained repeatedly about this to the Medical Staff Committee and Bill was told to get me to look after her properly. Fortunately, the other consultants had no complaint about my work and they didn't like her either. Having found no improvement she resigned. I regarded this as a victory for common sense. It was unusual for a house surgeon to cause a consultant to resign.

Although I was a house surgeon, medical emergencies came in through Casualty. One night I was called to a male with the classical symptoms of an acute coronary attack. He had been driving along the Common when he had acute chest pains radiating down his arm. Having heard this I first gave him a shot of morphine then the recommended emergency treatment for a heart attack and examined him. He was not sweaty, his BP was OK and to my eyes his ECG seemed normal. However, I said we would admit him because he had classic symptoms of a coronary. A short time later I had a telephone call from the ward; he had demanded another injection for his chest pain. When this was refused he got up and walked out. He was a middle class conman and drug addict at a time when morphine was difficult to get hold of. Addiction was not a condition with which I was familiar in 1964.

Because the Bolingbroke was a small hospital only those on call slept in. There was no social life. I was always relieved to get back to Walton Street to catch up on my sleep and resume a normal life the next week. The 1 in 2 rota was an intrusion in lifestyle but it had provided marvellous experience for me, being the equivalent of several jobs in one. I benefitted from this considerably and took much I had learned into my career.

Bill Heald also benefitted from his time there. he became an internationally recognised and honoured colo-rectal surgeon. He made a major contribution to improving the treatment and prognosis of colonic cancer and is still operating all over the world at the age of 77. He was made a professor and a CBE. A knighthood eluded him: a disgrace in my opinion.

12 Life as a Ship's Surgeon, Quite a Different World.

I owe this chapter of my life to Bill Heald. He had spent some time early in his career working as the surgeon on the mail ships of the Union Castle line, plying their trade between Southampton (Soton), Capetown and Durban. He owned a uniform and did the occasional relief trip. Bill's pal, and surgical colleague, John Kirkham, had previously worn this uniform, which had to be dry cleaned rapidly if it was to be used on the next trip. Bill was friendly with one of the Cayzers, the owners of Union Castle, and he had become the conduit for finding relief doctors from amongst his friends. He arranged for me to go on the Pretoria Castle after my full medical registration came through and I duly presented myself in Southampton in his uniform which was a passable fit but only just for I was bigger in the middle and shorter in height than Bill.

This was to be the ship's last trip as the Pretoria Castle as it was to change its name and ownership in Capetown to the Oranje of Safmarine in which the Cayzers also had a considerable holding. The ship, though quite old, was a delight, with its mahogany fittings and real style. It was over 20,000 tons and it made 20 knots for days on end carrying about 250 first class, 600-700 second class passengers and a crew of about 300. Richard Gordon looked after a dozen or so passengers and a small crew on a cargo ship totalling over 100. He had created a false impression of life as a ship's surgeon as I was soon to find out. Over the years I did several relief trips on Union Castle ships (ships have boats) and these long trips at sea have left me with warm memories for a way of life now gone. Now we rush to get ready for an overseas trip, spend hours in the airport, fly out, start work the next day often jet lagged and somehow complete a series of lectures, eat and drink late into the evening, travel the next day, give the same lectures the day after and return home worn out to catch up on the backlog of work at home. It took me weeks to recover from some lecture trips. What nicer way to get to South Africa than a twelve day voyage – two days to Las Palmas and ten days to Capetown, where most passengers got off and where we would take on South Africans and Americans making a coastal trip for their holiday. Two days in Capetown then up to Durban via East London and Port Elizabeth. Four days in Durban with shore leave to sightsee then make the return trip.

Using my accumulated annual leave, I made trips on the Pendennis Castle and a couple of short voyages on the Reina del Mer, the line's cruise liner, all still wearing Bill's uniform. These were 8-10 day cruises with multiple port visits and they lacked many of the pleasures of the mail ships. However, they offered education in another way of life, upon

R.M.S. PENDENNIS CASTLE

Working hard as ship's surgeon

which we may touch on later.

There were several surprises awaiting for me as a ship's surgeon, one being that as a senior departmental officer you are responsible for the ship's hygiene as well as the care of the passengers and crew. You captain the doctor's lifeboat. The ship's surgeon has the responsibility for deciding if the physical or mental illness renders the captain unfit for command. Since nearly every captain and chief engineer I sailed with were alcoholics, in a medical sense, this could have been difficult.

Alcohol was a problem for us all. The five departmental heads had an allowance from the Company with which we were expected to socialize with the passengers principally from the front of the ship. Mine was £32 a trip. Gin was 7/6d and whisky 10/- a bottle so it went a long way. If you ordered the wine at your table or a round of drinks in the passenger lounge, it was almost guaranteed that the passengers would reciprocate. The most dangerous time, however, was the daily Captain's Conference. We would meet about 11.00am and discuss the problems of the ship or passengers and plan how to deal with each one. Then we would go our separate ways to inspect the ship. I would visit the galley, toilets, crew quarters and check the water chlorination. I repeatedly upset the Head Chef by insisting he did not put cooked meats on the wet floor to cool and did not fill the wash basins with pots. I examined the fingernails of the cooks. We would then reconvene to the Captain's cabin to report. Before we departed for lunch we would have had up to five gins of the imperial measure. As each officer signed for his round, the conversation became more animated as we discussed various passengers. I always lunched in my cabin and retired to bed to recover, which is why you rarely see a senior officer in the early afternoon. In the early days of a voyage, I was often aware of a slight nausea but was not sure if this was because of the booze or the ship's motion. As it wore off, I found myself looking forward to the pre-lunch drink. A danger sign for me.

In the tropics, after dinner and visits to the public lounges, I would often climb to the storm bridge above the main bridge and sit gazing in alcoholic wonder at the stars above me. If the ship was making 20 knots and had a following wind of the same speed, the air was still and it was a wonderful experience, though poor preparation for any medical emergency which might present.

For the first time in my life I had to make a big adjustment for homosexuality. To my surprise, I quickly learned that the majority of the Purser's department of male stewards, cabin or restaurant or whatever, were gay – a description not then yet in use. As the Royal Navy frowned upon homosexuality, the merchant marine and, particularly passenger liners, attracted those who wished to live their way at sea. It was easy to determine where they slept for their bunk curtains, cabin decorations and drying underwear were evidence of their sexuality. At sea many of them had female names – one, my steward, who doubled as our hospital attendant, was a lovely blonde with long fingernails named Alice. He gave my female in-patients much appreciated massages. The senior officers were long accustomed to it all and on every round trip there would be a ship's concert and fancy dress competition for the crew, most of which was drag. It was easy to make mistakes – once I was leaning over the rail, with the Chief Officer, watching passengers disembark in Capetown. I said, 'Where are all those women coming from?' as I saw them going down the crew gang-way. 'Don't be silly Doc, that's the crew in drag!' he replied. The last syphilitic chancre I saw was on a crew member. Like an idiot, I asked him when he was last with a woman. He replied 20 years ago! He refused to name the source of his infection, so I said 'You had better tell this guy he may have a syphilis up his backside.' I put our patient off the ship as being medically unfit at the next main port. We had a number of AC/DCs who had a wife and family at home and a male lover at sea. Incidentally, the deck boys being heterosexual had the unpleasant habit of picking up gonorrhoea in Las Palmas. This would clear up with penicillin but they would re-infect themselves on the way back – penile strictures to come!

Large numbers of homosexuals within a small community can prove unstable. Groups form around a Queen who rules. There were two or three Queens on each ship. Love affairs were within the group and for individuals to leave that Queen, to move to another group or a lover outside of this group, or somehow offend a Queen was a risky business. All too often I would be called to find a crew member beaten up – quite savagely on occasion. Those who went ashore in drag also ran the risk of being beaten up by the locals as they made their way back if they became separated from their colleagues. Usually drunk or drugged they were easy meat. The worst beatings, however, occurred when they were lying drunk in a bunk when old scores or lost love affairs were settled, which often resulted in my sewing them up. Of course, there were never any witnesses.

The crew had the usual variety of physical and emotional illnesses, for which they sought medical help. On one ship the permanent doctor I relieved was also homosexual and obviously good to them. They didn't care much for me, for when they came with a cold, instead of putting them off work and giving them drugs, I told them off for wasting my time. On the other hand, the heterosexuals were glad to consult a heterosexual doctor. The crew surgery was at 8.00am with the passenger surgery starting at 9.00am. Then there were cabin visits to complete before the Captain's Conference. I always had a nurse with me as a chaperone.

There were a small but continuous number of injuries caused by moving machine parts but my most unpleasant memory was of being called from dinner, in my best whites, to the engine room. An engineer lay trapped by steel plates beneath the propeller shaft and was in pain and panicking. The noise and heat were stifling. He lay in an oily black sludge below the rotating shaft, trapped by the floor plate he had previously removed. Deciding he required sedation and pain relief urgently, I wondered how I could give it to him and still remain clean. There was no obvious way so I took off my jacket and shirt and slid down beside the shaft until I could find the engineer's arm. When he quietened down, his colleagues were able to manhandle the plate free whilst I kept him still. We got him out fairly easily and when I examined him all I could find were a few bruises. I sent my kit to the ship's Chinese laundrymen and returned to the social fray. Word got around and I became quite popular with the crew, even those with colds or those who put warm ham on a wet floor.

If sex reared its ugly head in the UK in the 60s, it was certainly well established at sea long before. Something seemed to happen to some women after they said good bye and the gangway was taken up. Is it the strangeness, the isolation from loved ones, the uniforms, the luxury accommodation and food, the alcohol, the throbbing engines, the freedom?

Whatever the cause, the results were manifest. The engineers knew about it too. I always enjoyed the spectacle of the ship leaving a main port after taking on new passengers. As band music played through the tannoy, the ship slowly left the quayside. Loved ones held onto ribbons or streamers until the increasing distance broke the contact. Tears, calls and waves added to the emotion. I used to watch this from the lifeboat deck and found myself surrounded by engineer officers. 'What's going on?' I asked. 'We are seeing who is crying the most,' they replied, meaning the women passengers. 'Why?' I queried. 'Because they usually require active sympathy,' was the answer. Sure enough! At the Captain's cocktail parties, held on the second and third nights, these women would be chatted-up, often with considerable success. Even if they were accompanied by their children there were places where these ladies enjoyed the sympathy offered by the officers and others, not least the cabins that somehow remained empty even when the ship was supposed to be full. A bottle of whisky for the steward could always provide accommodation. Officers were not supposed to have passengers in their cabins but this was largely ignored if the Captain was still active in this respect.

Some female first-class passengers played the slot machines continuously and others liaised with the young officers or the deck boys who serviced them for fun or a few bob. Some of these ladies became a problem and featured at the Captain's Conference. I was called more than once to see alleged rape cases. An irate parent noticing their daughter had disappeared would find her in her cabin, partially clothed or naked with a crew member in the wardrobe. The usual claim was assault by the crew member, but when I got the girl away from her parents, the truth usually came out. Amongst all the gays she was lucky to find someone straight.

All in all, I decided that I would never let a wife of mine travel by herself at sea. To this I would add particularly on a cruise liner after my clinical experience on the Reina del Mer, where the shortness of the cruise period seemingly increased the libido of all concerned, perhaps evidenced by the frequency of ladies presented with impacted tampons who I referred immediately to the nursing sister for assistance. Such problems were potentially the cause of acute toxic shock and required immediate correction.

Those ships were part of a huge business empire. In addition to passengers and cargo, they brought gold bullion from South Africa to the UK. If the company made money so it seems did a lot of other people, or at least it was rumoured they did. Did the Purser get backhanders from the merchants of Las Palmas? Did the Captain get a cut? How was it the Chief Steward and Chief Barman had Jaguar cars back in the UK? One day in the Captain's Conference, I told the Purser I had had about eight brandies after the previous evening's dinner and was still sober. 'OK' he said, 'I will tell him he's putting too much water in the bottle'. For the next few nights passengers and senior officers would be quickly intoxicated on un-doctored spirits until the watering started again. I used this knowledge on land where it appeared the landlords also watered the spirits, advising I would take their weak drink to the Weights & Measures if they did not give me a double to compensate for the water. I don't remember one of those I suspected refusing. Since most of the doctors needed the money, we also participated in a little racket. The company had a list of minimum charges to passengers for surgery or cabin visits. We made that the entry charge and charged additionally for services rendered. With a good storm in the Bay of Biscay and an injection of 50mgs of Phenergan, producing 4 hours of sleep, a great improvement in sea sickness and a tidy sum, I prayed for storms and beam seas.

On the Pretoria Castle there was one nursing sister, but on the larger ships such as the Pendennis Castle, there were two. I never did a cabin visit without a chaperone for you never knew what you would encounter. I did a call to see a local South African female with sunburn. She had forgotten the strength of the sun's rays because of the cool wind caused by the ship making 20 knots. The poor girl lay starkers on her bunk with first degree burns in all but three places. We took her into hospital to cool her down.

It was important after leaving Southampton and Capetown to find out what medical assistance was on board. The doctor's cocktail party was held on the third night after departure. All 'doctors' were invited along with persons thought to be allied to Medicine or Nursing. We would find out who were proper doctors and who were medical doctors, surgeons or obstetricians. If you were lucky there would be potential assistance available, but sometimes they were all theologians or PhDs.

Duties of the ship's doctor started before departure. It was wise to watch new passengers climb the gangway and for the medical staff to mix with the passengers as they came on board. The heavily pregnant, the obviously breathless or ill could be identified and approached. To put the ship into an unscheduled port to land a patient was costly and made one very unpopular with the Captain. Obstetrics at sea is not a good idea if avoidable. In Southampton, we called on an ill lady in her 80s lying on the bunk in a cabin with much younger relatives standing around her. It was easy to diagnose her broncho-pneumonia. 'She must go to hospital,' I said. The patient protested feebly. The story emerged that BOAC airline had refused to take her because of her illness and she wanted to get to Port Elizabeth to say farewell to her son before she died. I took the relatives outside and told them she would not make it to Port Elizabeth but might later on if she went to hospital now. I was entreated to take her. After discussing the patient with both of my nursing colleagues, I said the relatives must sign a paper which would detail my misgivings and poor prognosis but that, provided the patient came into our hospital from the start and the charges would be paid, we would do our best for her.

I could not claim to be anything other than a partially trained doctor and I really doubted our ability to save her. Perhaps we would find someone on board who could. So we set sail with her in our little hospital and we started antibiotics, physio and oxygen. We nursed her, cared for her, massaged her back and pressure areas (Alice nursed) and prayed for her. She improved a little. Alas there was not a medical doctor amongst the passengers. After Las Palmas, the patient continued to improve for a few days. I telexed her son, a Volkswagen agent in Port Elizabeth: 'Mother very ill. Please meet ship Capetown.' He replied, 'Will meet ship in Port Elizabeth,' I was both angry and saddened by this. His mother died peacefully 36 hours out of Capetown and we buried her at sea. In Capetown the British Consul came on board, as usual, to investigate the death at sea. He told us that the day our patient died her son had driven over a railway bridge into Port Elizabeth as a cloud of smoke and steam from a coal burning railway engine had obliterated visibility. The resultant crash had killed him. If he had come to Capetown he would still have been alive but probably cursing me for letting his mother die and so causing him an unnecessary journey – what a strange coincidence. I didn't feel sorry for him.

The average age of the 200-300 first class passengers was towards the top end. Many were pre or post convalescent or with terminal illness of some sort. I never forgave the GPs who told them, 'Now what you need is a breath of sea air!'

The rolling or pitching of the ship, alcohol, unusual exertion, dancing or just fun and games could result in a broken limb, banged head or collapse. Chest pain or shortness of breath could occur at any time. Cabin calls in first class were generally pleasant but in the lower decks the atmosphere could be stifling, particularly in bad weather and it was difficult to examine patients lying in a bunk. Every now and again a passenger would die and because there was no suitable place to keep them, they were buried at sea either during the next dinner or breakfast. Amazingly the news would get about and people with cameras would be hanging over the rails looking down on the small deck behind the medical quarters. The senior officers would parade in their uniforms and the relatives would stand beside the sailcloth enclosed corpse laid on a board covered by the Union Jack next to the rail. The old tradition of the bosun sewing the corpse into canvas was still followed, even to the last stitch in nose. He would get a bottle of whisky for doing it. Even that stitch did not stop me from having a qualm or two as the board was tipped to commit the body to the deep. I knew there was no turning back. Company policy was for the engines to be gradually slowed and finally stopped so that the weighty fire bars inside the canvas would take the body to the deep. Not every Captain followed this policy. One, rumoured to have a woman in Capetown, always kept the ship at full cruising speed so that the propeller had the final say in how deep the corpse went. He assuaged his guilt by toasting the departed. After the relatives had taken their leave, we put on our caps and marched into my cabin where Alice was ready with the gin and tonics on a tray. Once as we entered the Captain sniffed 'Doctor', he said 'have you got a woman in here?'

'No sir, it's only Alice,' I replied

'Oh that's OK,' he said. Alice used Chanel No.5. The Captain raised his glass – 'To the departed.' Our drinks went down in one gulp and everybody went on their way. I paid for the drinks from my allowance.

Despite this, I believe burial at sea to be highly commended. It was quickly arranged, cheap, simple, clean and moving – emotionally as well as literally. The diagnosis of the cause of sudden death could be a problem for the death certificate but more often than not, there was a history of illness to assist me.

Not all funerals went well. One evening I was called to see a boy about 10 years old who had fallen out of his top bunk, striking his head on the dressing table. He was sleepy and weepy with a headache and had a soft swelling on his temple. However, his vital signs, his pupils and limb reflexes were normal. I told the mother that I could not find anything other than the bruise but she should keep an eye on him and if he vomited or his headache worsened she should call us. Some hours later we were called; he had vomited. Again, I could not find neurological abnormality but I said we had to have him in hospital where we would put him on head injury observation. I briefed both Sisters and arranged to be called if the pupil size or pulse rate altered. After a final check I went to bed. About 3.00 am Sister woke me up telling me the child was fitting. His body was rigid and arched and I knew immediately his condition was desperate. I carried him in my pyjamas and dressing gown into the operating theatre and without bothering about sterilisation made an incision in the swelling of his temple. I found a small 3cm long skull fracture on his temple and went through it with a manual trephine. It was the first and last time I did this and I was surprised how quickly the trephine went through. Underneath there was a mass of blood clot. As I started to remove it his heart arrested and breathing ceased. He had cloned his brain stem and died.

We were all deeply shocked and the worst part I remember was telling his mother. She became hysterical. As the boy was buried we had to restrain her to stop her throwing herself after him. As we were a few days out of Capetown, we kept her in hospital after she attempted to go through her cabin window. I didn't feel much better. How had we allowed this to happen? I was certain that I had not been fooled by the pupils and limb reflexes. The pupil and pulse chart showed no abnormality. I opened his skull before we wrapped him up and nearly half of the brain cavity was full of blood clot. He must have had localising signs. I was left with the possibility that the nurse had fallen asleep and had not done the observations and that the chart had been filled in subsequently. Would we have saved him if he had demonstrated signs of increasing inter-cranial pressure? I was not a neurosurgeon, nor had I done a trephining before. We did not have an anaesthetist although I might have stopped the bleeding and decompressed his pressure. The last place you want to rupture your middle meningial artery is at sea, a long way from land. The British Consul arranged for a neurosurgeon from Capetown to come to the ship to talk things over with me. He kindly suggested that intracranial bleeding in children can be sudden and catastrophic. Now in my 80s, I still think about this boy and wonder if we could have saved him. The sudden death of a child affects not only the parents.

Apart from these catastrophes, life on board was a pleasure. As a senior officer I had my own table in the first class dining room at which a number of well known names became familiar. The quality of the cuisine and wine was of a standard I have rarely matched since. Work in the morning, sun or sleep in the afternoon, some work in the evening followed by a good dinner with delightful people and we were being paid!

Over the years, I had three return trips to South Africa and two or three on the cruise liner. Marriage in 1970 ended my sea faring. I remain grateful for having had the opportunity to sample a seafaring life that is no longer available.

13 Senior Registrar- A Training Post?

I had been engaged to Elizabeth for about two years. We were due to marry on an already arranged date, which would follow my return from sea. I returned to the UK to find that Elizabeth had broken off the engagement. She had met somebody with an XK Jaguar. My world collapsed and for some time I was distraught – a broken heart was an easy self-diagnosis. I had to go up to Newcastle which made it virtually impossible to attempt a reconciliation. I also had the emotional problem of jealousy, juvenile though it might have been, with her sleeping with someone else. I therefore went up to Newcastle with a troubled mind which left me less than prepared to put up with what was to follow. I was hardly in a romantic mood and a few unfortunate girls did not benefit from my not seeking a permanent relationship. I don't remember this time with any pleasure and it took my psyche a long time to recover. I regret the unhappiness I caused Maureen in particular.

After I finished my house jobs in 1964, but before I went to sea for the first time, I had reluctantly applied for a senior registrar post in the Royal Victoria Infirmary Newcastle (known as the RVI). I really did not want to go back to the North East but I needed a job. Because I was not overly keen on returning to the North East, I was somewhat carefree with my sense of humour and Professor Howe told me later that I nearly blew the interview. I was to wish I had.

A senior registrar is a post designed to enable a junior to become a senior doctor or consultant by giving them increasing responsibility for diagnosis and treatment. The senior registrar relies upon consultants to teach the more difficult or the latest procedures so that he could confidently commence the post of a consultant when appointed. I did not get that in Newcastle. During the first few months of my appointment I found that I was on my own, supported by a likable competent resident dental officer, Peter McAndrew, for Howe, my consultant, was recovering from emergency abdominal surgery. I relied upon my previous experience of general surgery and the knowledge gained in oral and maxilla facial injury from Tom Battersby, Norman Rowe and Ian Heslop. My operative skills quickly returned. I had attended the conferences of my Specialist Association during my medical student days and I knew techniques had moved on significantly since I was a registrar. Facial fractures more frequently were treated by open direct fixation of fractures with wire or metal plates and screws. Plaster head caps were no more. The correction of facial deformity was also developing rapidly with techniques involving both jaws and the cheekbones.

Without consultant supervision I was left to develop my skills very much by self-teaching, practice and going to conferences. We soon cornered the facial injuries that came to the RVI, assisted by a good dental mechanic, Harry Charlton, sadly now deceased. Life outside of the RVI was fun. I purchased a semi in a good area of Gosforth for £3.5K and became proficient in cooking and housekeeping. Without the southern traffic jams, I drove over Northumberland and Durham in my MG, often with the top down, and loved the country except when there were funeral pyres of cattle burning during the outbreak of food and mouth disease. My mother lived nearby in Sunderland.

After two years it was clear that I was not going to learn anything more of value at the RVI. I would have applied for another job in the North East had one been available. Three consultant advertisements appeared for Stoke on Trent, Nottingham and Cardiff. I was shortlisted for each one. Stoke in the Potteries was not particularly attractive. Nottingham was a busy place of which I had experience, but Tom had died when I was at medical school and a singly qualified oral surgeon had taken his post. Cardiff was a job in the new dental teaching hospital with oral surgery beds in the general hospital. The new medical teaching hospital was a large hole in the ground, covered by a steel girder structure. A teaching post was attractive to me and new hospital buildings a large carrot, for our department in the RVI had been built to take World War I casualties.

An unhappy coincidence was that all interviews were in the same week. I was advised by Professor Howe that Brian Cooke, the Dean at Cardiff, was a difficult person and I should not apply. The Stoke appointment interview was on the Monday. Brian Hales, the incumbent dental consultant and a good friend of Tom Battersby's and sympathetic to me, rang me to tell me on Sunday that the likely appointment at Stoke would be Geoff Manning, also doubly qualified and who had worked there previously. That was OK but Brian also told me that he was to be the Royal College of Surgeons' external assessor at Nottingham and that the plastic Surgeon, Wynn Williams, and the incumbent dental consultant did not want a medically qualified appointment, particularly me. I also learned from another source that the Dean of the Dental School in Cardiff favoured a candidate who was not medically qualified, from Guy's, his old hospital. The immediate future looked bleak. I failed to get either of the first two jobs despite having good interviews. I had major anxieties about Cardiff, not being either a Guy's man or Welsh but on the panel there was a doubly qualified oral surgeon from North Wales, Gordon Hardman. He dominated my interview and later told me how he scuppered the Dean's effort to appoint the Guy's candidate. I was told that the Committee would advise the board of Governors to appoint me. Yippee! I had a job with potential and

I would become a Welshman. After all there were five Hopkins in the Newcastle telephone book and five pages of them down in Cardiff.

My confirmation of the appointment soon arrived and I started my final three months in Newcastle. I was not sorry to leave. Having sold my house and arranged to rent one owned by the Board of Governors, close to the hospital, I set off for Cardiff in my MG. As usual in my career, I missed all of the later improvements to the consultant contract and had to fund all removal expenses myself.

14 Consultant in Cardiff – A Fresh Start in an Alien Environment.

I took up my post in Cardiff on my 36th birthday and was appointed without a job description or a formal time table. Professor Cooke had decided that a consultant was required to do the donkey work in the department so that his senior lecturer, John Wolfe, could teach and research. Almost on my first day it became clear why he wanted the single qualified Guy's man for the job. I was summoned to see him. 'I want you to take over the local extraction department,' he said. 'I'm sorry,' I said 'I have been appointed to be a consultant oral surgeon and that is what I propose to be, not a dentist doing dental extractions. This may have been the second time the powerful Brian Cooke had been rebuffed. When he first opened the School he had recruited a Guy's man to run the oral surgery department who resigned after a short time and went back to London. The job then lay empty for some time. Despite the earlier warnings about Cooke, the lure of the new buildings and teaching hospital job had been too strong for me. I was determined to be an NHS consultant. As a non-academic consultant I was not considered suitable by Cooke to teach the dental students.

Cooke publicly spoke of consultants as 'donkeys'. He could not understand why I did operations more than once. Anybody who did not research was a waste of time, in his opinion. He considered that I was a donkey who should do his master's bidding. He and I did not hit it off. I then discovered I transgressed his instructions when I dictated letters to my secretary with my office door shut. Cooke assumed everybody but him was a sex maniac and insisted if a male and female were in the same room together, the door must be open! My dislike of dental academia was increased by what I endured in those early months!

John Wolfe was senior lecturer and honorary consultant with whom I hoped to work. He had had a brilliant academic undergraduate career, obtaining the gold medal of London University as a medical student. There was a 'visiting' Consultant oral Surgeon, John Gibson, who came from the Plastic and Jaw Unit at Chepstow. He was of the old school and in the Oral Surgery Club. I discovered that all but the simplest jaw fractures were referred from the Cardiff Royal Infirmary (CRI) and the Morriston Hospital Swansea to Chepstow, where they were admitted by the plastic surgeons and kept for weeks filling beds unnecessarily. Gibson fitted the cap splints or wired the teeth together. He did not cut skin or repair mid-face fractures. There was one shining light in Cardiff, the senior registrar Khursheed Moos, doubly qualified. He told me he had been in Cardiff for two years and considered it a waste of his time. He told me that he was already applying for consultant posts but when he learned I proposed to change things he said he would stay.

One of my first tasks was to meet my essential medical and surgical colleagues. John Newham, FRCS, was the consultant in charge of the accident and emergency department in the CRI. He was South African and we got on famously after I related my South African connections. I said we would be pleased to take all the facial injuries he cared to refer and soon that became all of them. Alas Morriston continued to refer fractures to Chepstow.

It was not long before the plastic surgeons at Chepstow were complaining and they put up a notice in the CRI Casualty advising what facial injuries should be referred to them. I went to see John Newham who had it removed. About eighteen months later I was asked to attend a meeting, arranged by the Professor of Surgery, Pat Forest, with the senior plastic surgeon, Len Schofield. At that time discussions were underway about moving the Chepstow unit to Cardiff. Forest requested Schofield to open discussion. He said he was aware that I had been treating facial injuries in the CRI and he was content I continued to be involved in them. All such patients would be admitted into plastic beds in the new unit and the plastic surgeons would refer cases to me that they considered suitable. I could hardly believe my ears. I replied that I was a consultant and that I would accept patients referred to me by anybody, including the casualty consultants of the CRI and that I was responsible to the General Medical Council and the Courts for the standard of my work and not to them, and that I saw little point in continuing these discussions any further. With my heart in my mouth, I left the room. Effectively, however, that was the end of the plastic problem. I learnt of their continued sour grapes from friendly sources on several occasions but by then my position in Cardiff had strengthened, whilst theirs had weakened. Finally, their Unit was transferred to Swansea not Cardiff, much against their wishes. I was by then Chairman of the Medical Staff Committee and on the Area Health Authority Management Team. The plastic surgeons blamed me when in reality I had nothing to do with the final decision which was taken by the Welsh Office; I certainly did nothing to assist them. The petrochemical and steel industries were in West Wales. The oral surgery and maxillofacial care was updated by new consultant appointments.

The usual supply and sources of facial injuries continued to come to the Cardiff Royal Infirmary. There was heavy industry in the area in addition to mining. Underground roof falls could cause grotesque injury. I was called on a Sunday afternoon – a miner was on the way in with several injuries. He arrived with his face flattened and crushed and his clothes totally covered in coal dust. He needed an immediate tracheotomy to safeguard his airway. He was transferred to the operating table where I did the trache, using local analgesia before he was undressed. He was then anaesthetised, stripped of his filthy clothes and washed. Below neck, his upper body was covered in Catholic religious tattoos but below the belt region was replaced by pornography. The one area that appeared free of decoration was his penis. 'Sister' I questioned, 'Is there anything on that?'. She straightened it and we could see a printed word that looked like GOMANGO. 'What on earth is that' I said, and then 'Sister give it a pull' GO MAN GO became obvious. During the lengthy operation to repair his face, I noticed several senior sisters visiting the lower end of the patient. News travels fast in a hospital.

There are several ways of making a surgical reputation, some essentially based on good fortune. JPR Williams, a medical student at St. Mary's, was rapidly establishing a demigod reputation in Wales as an international full back. Scotland versus Wales at the Arms Park saw me in the old south stand. Williams was involved in an incident with Peter Brown the Scottish captain. Later an up and under kick saw the Scottish pack fall on top of Williams, who was now groggy. He then had to tackle Billy Steel, the Scottish winger, who was travelling at speed. Williams went down and stayed down until carried off on a stretcher. When the match ended I went to the CRI where I met Peter McAndrew, late of Newcastle and now my registrar. He said that JPR had a fractured upper jaw. I went into Casualty where his father, a general practitioner, stood beside him. I examined JPR and the radiographs. His upper jaw had a segmental fracture of the front of the tooth bearing component which had been driven downwards and backwards. This resulted in Williams being unable to put his jaws together or speak clearly.

After examining JPR, I told them that there was a good chance I could get the teeth back in position using local analgesia but if I could not shift the bone, a general anaesthetic would be required. It was agreed that I proceed. Peter injected every major sensory nerve in the area. When all was numb, I slowly applied increasing pressure with my bent figures upon the back of the displaced segment. What I wished to avoid was ejecting the whole piece out of the mouth with his father watching. With counter pressure, slowly the jaw was realigned. 'Bite hard,' I ordered and JPR bit it into its final position. I wired on an arch bar quickly to hold it in place and told JPR to go back to the hotel to bathe and change. I suggested a few beers might reduce the expected discomfort along with a couple of paracetamols. I was then introduced to the hype of the press and celebrity. The newspapers reported that JPR had talked the doctor into using local and letting him out of hospital so that he could go back to the hotel and party. It made good press but irritated me. JPR set the record straight in his subsequent autobiography and I became the guy who repaired JPR, which did me no harm.

In the 1960-70s days of amateur rugby, it was the Welsh national game and Wales were dominant. To play first class rugby and achieve international recognition was the aim of many a school boy. This could lead to extreme behaviour. Glamorgan Wanderers, a first class club, was to play the touring Australian team. In a routine club game their winger Iliff received a blow which resulted in a severely depressed fracture of his cheekbone. At operation it came up without difficulty and was stable without requiring an open reduction. When he came to the clinic to have his sutures out I told him he should not play rugby for a couple of months. He was forlorn. 'Could I train?' he asked. 'Yes, but you must avoid all physical contact. No touch rugby or tackling practice,' I replied. Iliff came to see me a couple of weeks later. He begged me to allow him to play against the Australians. I could see the desperation in his eyes – the pleading. I told him of the consequences of refracturing his cheek – the almost certain need for open reduction and fixation, the possibility of damage to his eye. He accepted my warnings but still asked for permission to play. I did not have the courage to say no. I said 'You must accept all responsibility for your own actions or injury. I will look after you if it goes wrong.' A month after his original injury he played against Australia. His team lost, but he did not re-fracture his cheekbone and he had played the game!

Before long titanium bone plates replaced steel plates to give rigid support to fractures. They were used on the orbital rims, mid-face and lower jaw. A club rugby player had a fractured, displaced lower jaw bone which was reduced and fixed by me with a small plate held by two screws at each end. As usual we mobilized the lower jaw so that he could eat softish foods. I gave him the usual advice to stop playing for the next two months. However, his side were doing well in a competition. Ten days later I saw his name in the local paper included in his team to play two weeks after his original injury. That Saturday he was back in the CRI. He had been punched early on and his jaw bone had gone! When I went in through the original wound I found the screws still holding but the plate was bent in the middle by about 45º. We flattened it out and put it back after realigning the teeth and bone. All was well but he did not play again that season. I was mightily impressed by the strength of a small titanium plate and four screws, as well as the determination of rugby players.

In the late 60s Wales invariably beat the home teams. Tickets could usually be obtained from the Hall Porter at the CRI and as I sat in the old South stand shouting my support for England, I realised I was almost

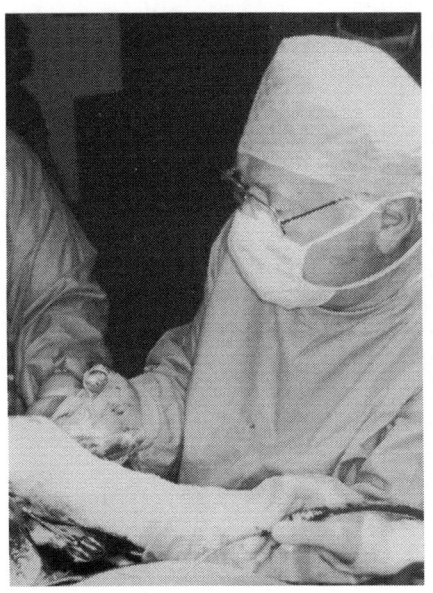

Operating: A rib graft to the temporomandibular joint.
Photo: Andrew Ezias

alone in doing so. One lady sitting in front of me asked me not to make so much noise. She was in a group of wives and girlfriends of English players. I told them they should not sit so quietly taking defeat like ladies. We used to meet in the nearby Angel Hotel for post-match drink and discussion. After one England last minute loss, I put up with a lot of leg pulling in the crowded upstairs bar. A door opened and in sauntered the England team led by Rob Andrews. Silence descended as they strutted through to their dining room. Their pride was overwhelming despite losing and they were accorded respect by all in the bar simply because they were rugby players. It made my hair tingle on the back of my neck. I wanted to stand and sing 'God Save the Queen', but self-preservation won the day.

My surgical discipline owes its origin to World War I and the initial inadequate treatment of missile derived facial injuries. The principles of repair of facial fractures were established then though techniques develop even to this day. Explosives and missiles often caused the loss of soft tissues and bone requiring specialized repair, but my clinical experience related to civilian injuries from industrial, road traffic, falls, domestic incidents and assaults. Le Fort, a military surgeon of Napoleonic times, had dropped cannon balls onto the faces of dead soldiers. After dissecting their faces, he described three lines of fracture in the mid-face: the Le Fort 1, a horizontal fracture of the upper jaw separating it from the nasal and antral sinus skeleton; Le Fort 2, was the pyramidal fracture of a one piece upper jaw and nasal skeleton, whilst the Le Fort 3 included one or both cheekbones with the mid facial fractures. In reality, mid-faced fractures were always more complicated than single lines but his descriptions were useful for communication. Because of the angulations of the base of skull, the face could be driven inwards, downwards or sidewards. It was quite common for the lower jaw to be fractured in more than one place and sometimes the frontal bone would be shattered. Such injuries could have severe consequences, e.g. blindness in one or both eyes, or tearing of the dura mater or brain membrane, allowing infection to gain access to the brain through the nose. Displacement of either jaw altered the dental occlusion so that patients could not speak correctly, masticate and, of course, the 'dish face' of a middle facial fracture was a severe cosmetic impairment.

By the time I was a consultant, Plaster of Paris head caps, initially used for fixation of facial fractures, had been replaced. Firstly they were replaced by halo frames; these consisted of a metal ring held onto the skull by screws and then by four bone pins screwed into the lateral bone just above the eyebrow and then the mandible, to which a metal 'box' frame was fixed to immobilize the jaws. Bone pins were used for comminuted fractures.

Today the use of halos and pins has been eliminated, by multiple open reductions and plating; time consuming but effective in that the reduction is accurate and there is no external metal to create a nuisance and problems with sleeping.

This work required skilled anaesthetic support and co-operation, and the insertion of nasal or oral airways when the face was crushed if a tracheotomy was to be avoided. Such patients usually had their jaws fixed together post operatively which meant the patient initially had to breathe through a nasal airway which had to be kept unblocked by the skilled nurses using suction in intensive care units.

Two patients remain in my memory. A young six or seven year old boy was run over by a trailer pulled by a tractor, driven by his father. He had been admitted to the children's ward under the care of the orthopaedic surgeons who, in those far off days, also looked after head injuries. When I examined him about a week after admission, I found him to have midface and multiple frontal bone fractures. There was a four inch oblique scar extending from the mid line over his forehead and his eyes were widely separated but still functional. The trailer wheel had squashed his face. In theatre we gained access to his forehead by lifting the scalp forehead downwards and forwards. The frontal bone of the forehead was a collection of multiple and impacted pieces of bone. Each piece was identified and wired back into its correct position, apart from an area between the upper orbits which was essential to fix the orbits in the correct position. We could not find this bone and ultimately we pulled the orbits together with wire. The result was reasonable; although the gap between the eyes was slightly increased he did not have double vision. I learned, subsequently, that a junior doctor had taken the boy to theatre to explore the forehead wound without consulting his superiors and finding pieces of loose bone he had thrown them away!

The second patient is an example of unfortunate consequence of facial injuries falling into the wrong hands. We had a call from the British Embassy in Paris: 'Could you take a Welsh female who had been in a road traffic accident?' Her boyfriend had filled the car tank up with petrol and had driven out of the garage onto the wrong side of the road straight into a lorry. When the patient was admitted into the University Hospital of Wales, I was horrified by the badly scarred, grotesque face of an allegedly young woman. After the accident she had been flown to Paris and admitted into Hospital Nekker, under ENT surgeons, where she had had at least three operations under general anaesthesia. It appeared to me that her face was collapsed and the facial soft tissues lacked underlying skeletal support. That, coupled with greasy unkempt hair made her a sorry picture. We examined the radiographs sent with her, the quality of which was poor, but even they suggested all was not well. We sent her for a new radiographic examination. With the results and our clinical examination we were able to assess her problem.

She had sustained a bilateral fracture of the mandibular condyles and oblique anterior fracture of the lower jaw with loss of a lower incisor tooth. Both cheekbones had been fractured, in addition to her mid-face. She had a classic Le Fort 3 with a triple fracture of the mandible. Unfortunately, our French colleagues had fixed the lower jaw in its collapsed state not realising the fracture of the jaw joints had allowed the jaw to move posteriorly. A metal arch bar had been used which closed the space of the missing tooth. The upper jaw had been fixed to the collapsed posterior-positioned lower jaw. Internal fixation had been used to immobilize the face but, unfortunately, the wire on one side had been inserted into broken cheekbone which had been pulled downwards and inwards as the wire was tightened. The other cheekbone had been correctly fixed to the skull but the wire to the lower jaw had been passed outside of the cheekbone so that as it was tightened the cheekbone had been pressed inwards.

Her three operations had left her facial skeleton collapsed and her soft tissues unsupported. We requested pre-accident photographs and they showed an attractive young lady with good cheekbones and a lovely smile. After getting the patient's agreement and with the agreement of her parents (was her boyfriend killed?) we took her to theatre and removed all fixation, re-fractured and repositioned her mid facial skeleton having first returned the lower jaw to its correct anatomical shape and position. Anterior skull fixation kept her face in a forward position until the fractures stabilised.

The final result, plus hair washing and make up, produced a dramatic improvement. I used her photographic slides for many lectures to reinforce the message that people treating facial injuries needed to understand the dental occlusion, the mechanics of facial fractures and their repair.

These lectures, which I gave over South Wales and the English border, were important in establishing my reputation with both the dental and medical professions. Having secured the facial trauma I had to build up on elective surgical practice. I approached a Cardiff orthodontic consultant, Derek Seel, who was appointed shortly after me, and we set up a joint clinic. I soon had a regular supply of his orthodontic patients with unerupted teeth requiring removal or transplantation, or skeletal jaw discrepancies requiring surgical correction. A similar clinic was agreed with the Professor of Prosthetic Dentistry, John Bates, who in due course was replaced by his senior lecturer Derrick Stafford. From the prosthetic clinic came a steady number of patients who, having lost their teeth in early adulthood, subsequently lost the bone that had supported the teeth. The lower jaw was the principal culprit but the upper jaw could also be flat so that their dentures were non-retentive or painful. Tom Battersby had earlier started my interest in this problem. In addition, there was a constant stream of patients referred directly to me from general dental and medical practitioners with a variety of problems, not always surgical.

By the time I was appointed there were several techniques for the correction of mandibular enlargement, which produced functional and cosmetic problems. The first patients arrived from the orthodontic clinic and were on my waiting list. Khursheed Moos, my senior registrar, and I had read the literature but few papers included the operative detail on how to deal with the technical complications. Having acquired the necessary instruments we worked out what to do and got on with it. Often we took the clinical papers or books into theatre to remind us of what to do. We rapidly developed the necessary operative skills by working together. I was sorry to lose him to a consultant appointment in Stratford upon Avon after a year. (He later moved to the Canniesburn Plastic & Jaw Unit, Scotland to earn a worldwide reputation and a Professorship.)

All these patients were first examined in the combined oral surgery/ orthodontic clinic to determine what and where was the cause of the facial asymmetry. Orthodontic correction of the occlusion, where possible, was completed prior to surgery so that the teeth could occlude correctly at operation.

Initially, almost all techniques were for reducing the size of the lower jaw which would correct the malocclusion but spoil the facial profile if the disproportion lay in the mid-face. Hugo Obwegeser of Zurich described an osteotomy of the mandibular ramus which was split vertically as opposed to being sectioned, allowing the jaw to be taken forward or backward as required but still maintaining posterior bone to bone contact. I listened to him describe this innovative intro-oral operation at a conference and read his literature. It seemed easy to do! We managed to get the special instruments and soon a suitable patient presented – a young man with a huge lower jaw protrusion requiring well over a one centimetre push back.

Our patient was keen to have the operation because of his functional and aesthetic problems with eating. We warned him his lower lip would probably be numb for a few weeks afterwards but he still agreed to proceed. Many surgical authors describe new surgical techniques as if they were problem free. They omit the difficulties to be faced during their learning curve. Obwegeser was one of these.

The first problem I discovered was how little room there seemed to be to accommodate the instruments and work at the back of the mouth. Secondly, it was not easy to visualize the bone as it was being sectioned using the surgical burr, so that there was the danger of cutting too deeply. Having completed three osteotomies and joined them up, I then used the special chisel to split the ramus of the mandibular in the vertical plane. Instead of splitting it shattered into several pieces and, to my horror, I saw that the mandibular neurovascular bundle or nerve had been sectioned. I was further horrified when I did the same thing on the other side! I literally wanted to walk away. I imagined, not for the first or the last time, my career was over. After repairing the nerve bundles as best I could, we put the jaw backwards and immobilized it in the correct dental occlusion with the upper jaw. I left the theatre dejected, convinced I had given this patient a numb lower lip probably for life. My career in Cardiff surely was finished.

The good news was that when the swelling resolved, the patient was delighted with his vastly new improved appearance which for him was a bonus. We left him with jaws wired together for a couple of weeks longer than usual and when we mobilised his jaws at eight weeks, bone union had occurred. He had coincidently lost his fat belly because of his limited diet and generally looked good. The bad news was his numb lower lip, but he denied this was a major problem. I made the decision never to do this particular operation again. He was always upbeat on his visits. It was a major surprise for me when a year later he told me that his lower lip sensation was now normal. I tested his lip and he could feel light touch! 'I can tell you now,' I said, 'I never thought it would recover,' He replied, 'I always knew it would. Every Sunday in chapel we prayed for my lip to get better and it has.' I thought if God is on my side there is no limit to what I can do.

It was not too long before I was repeatedly using this valuable technique and as experience works wonders, soon I could complete the procedure within the hour. With hindsight, my first patient's jaw was too thin for first time success without the guidance of an experienced colleague. This was a long term product of my wasted years in Newcastle and the difficulty to get study leave.

Techniques for moving the upper jaw backwards or forwards were now emerging which meant mid-face abnormalities could be corrected. If the upper jaw was sectioned horizontally from its nasal base, it could be moved upwards, downwards or forwards. Sectional osteotomies of the upper jaw were required occasionally and were usually staged. I performed a double osteotomy of an upper jaw, moving the front backwards and one side inwards after dropping the jaw downwards so that I could cut it from above, whilst leaving an intact blood supply from the soft palate. My published paper was the first in the literature. It was not too long before we did a Le Fort 3 osteotomy, bringing the upper jaw and the nose forward in one block. This patient had an unfortunate facial appearance and had long been subjected to verbal abuse from school children in Merthyr Tydfil. After the operation she told us the children asked her, 'Were you Vera?'

Obesity has always been a clinical problem and occasionally we were requested, by a physician, to wire an obese patient's jaw together for several weeks. Considerable weight loss did occur in the first few weeks but after a year of jaw freedom almost all patients had put their weight back on. I stopped doing the procedure.

All surgeons encounter problems during operations, some with or without complications. Early in my consultant career I was enlarging a lower jaw so that it would occlude with the upper jaw. The technique involved bilateral submandibular incisions to expose the posterior part of the lower jaw which were then sectioned vertically. Bone taken from the hip crest was shaped and inserted in the osteotomy to hold the front part of the lower jaw forward. I fashioned the hip bone and inserted it without difficulty on one side. As I shaped the remaining bone graft it shot out of my slippery rubber covered fingers onto the floor! The anaesthetist kicked it back towards me! I blasphemed more than a little and carefully lifted it up and put it in saline. I decided I would not reopen the hip but requested Sister to wash the graft carefully. We put it in place, relying upon antibiotics to prevent infection. It worked well! It confirms that cleanliness in hospitals and particularly operating theatres is essential. Mention of our theatre sister prompts me to say that efficient theatre staff are crucial to effective surgery. They can make life impossible for the surgeon or they can make surgery easier. It really is teamwork – surgeons, anaesthetists and theatre staff. When things were going well I often found myself singing, much to the annoyance of nearby surgical colleagues.

Bone grafts from the hip crest or ribs were harvested, not only to enlarge the jaws but to reconstruct defects and replace ankylosed or solid jaw joints. I did a joint reconstruction on a young girl whose joint had been destroyed by rheumatoid arthritis – Still's disease. Her jaw not only did not open but the normal side deviated significantly to the affected side. The rib graft was taken composed of rib topped by cartilage. Sometimes normal growth continued in the young. Years later, when I was Chairman of Glan-y-Mor Trust, an attractive staff nurse came up to me on a ward in Neath General and asked if I remembered her. I must have looked blank so she told me she was the young girl on whom I had done a joint reconstruction. She was my old patient. Her jaw was symmetrical, opened well and she was now an attractive adult with inactive rheumatoid disease.

Within a short time, my surgical practice encompassed not only impacted teeth, cysts, lumps and bumps, but also the salivary glands, tumours, oral cancer and the range of facial disproportion. The reconstruction of soft tissue defects then involved swinging the soft tissue forehead or the anterior cheek up into the mouth. These techniques are now history, replaced by composite grafts complete with a blood supply. I also developed pre-prosthetic surgery for both jaws to enable those who had insufficient bone to wear dentures. I became an international authority and travelled the western world. My published book (A Colour Atlas of Pre-prosthetic Oral Surgery. Wolfe 1987) sold well for a short time. However, ultimately titanium implants replaced much of this work.

My clinical reputation in Cardiff was enhanced by a lecture I gave to a packed Cardiff Medical Society entitled 'To consider the proverb 'Beauty is but skin deep' ". I showed beauty owed more to bone than skin. One patient I demonstrated whose upper jaw had failed to grow, looked desperately ugly with a terrible haircut and collapsed mid-face. She looked so different post-operatively that someone in the audience exclaimed it was not the same patient. I was delighted to correct him. This girl taught us a lesson. When she returned to work she had two abortions and made an attempt on her life. She had not learned to say 'no' and she could not cope with contraception. After that, every patient was seen by a psychologist pre-operatively, to identify potential problems and help us decide if they were suitable for surgery.

I was not the only consultant to be surprised now and again. A child presented with an unusual generalised destructive lesion surrounding the roots of his deciduous teeth and underlying permanent tooth germs. I removed much of this soft tissue and the histological diagnosis was of a rare pathology histiocytosis X, a potentially lethal disease. I discovered we had a paediatrician, Dr. Percy Bray, who had published papers on the subject.

I referred the patient to him and awaited his reply. Some weeks later, as I passed him in the corridor, I asked him why I had not heard about her. He looked very uncomfortable as he told me his junior staff had accidentally injected the child with several times the minimal lethal dose of a cytotoxic drug. The child had been most unwell for a time without white blood cells, but she had recovered and the multiple lesions of her pathology had disappeared! She remained clear so far. 'Wonderful' I said. 'You must write her up. Perhaps you weren't treating your patients with sufficient therapy. You might lose some but you might save more.' He was not impressed by my argument and kept it under wraps but progress can come from mistakes.

Medicine has its ups and downs for clinicians. The downs require a clinician develop a clinical hardness to protect their own psyche and assist them in making the correct clinical decisions. Happily, there are also patients who will bring great satisfaction. A married couple in their 30s presented in my private rooms. The wife had developed a gradual increasing limitation of opening of her jaw, the cause of which was not discovered in two hospitals in the South of England. She could barely open more than 1cm. A standard radiograph did not show an obvious cause so I suggested we should investigate her at the University Hospital of Wales. An obvious complication was her 6 month pregnancy.

I spoke to my radiology colleague, Dr. Arnold Williams, who performed specialist investigations and he obtained marvellous slices of her skull base which demonstrated a lesion invading the temporo mandibular jaw joint and the ascending ramus of the lower jaw. Needle biopsy proceeded the diagnosis of a slow growing low grade cancer of the salivary gland. We agreed to consult an obstetrician for a decision as to when he considered our patient's third child could be safely delivered. The eighth month was decided. I then had an opinion from our oncologist, who recommended radiotherapy post-operatively.

One month after the child had been safely delivered, I resected the tumour and the whole of the posterior lower jaw. We prevented the jaw deviating by fixing it to the upper jaw but could not put in a metallic bar to hold the jaw or attempt a reconstruction because of the radiotherapy. This resulted in the replaced skin flap collapsing into a deep cavity. After completing the radiotherapy, supervised by Dr. Michael Kemp, my prosthetic colleague Derek Stafford (now Professor), constructed a facial prosthesis which was retained by adhesives and filled in the cavity, enabling the patient to mix with the public without them noticing. Every Christmas I have had a card containing the photograph of three young adults sent by my old patient who remains alive and well today having had liver secondaries, and others, removed by general surgeons and facial reconstruction by colleagues at Bart's Hospital.

Consultants also become involved in medico legal work for insurance companies and the pro-legal profession. I was requested by the insurance company from a town in Pembrokeshire to report on an elderly retired nurse who had tripped over a flagstone; landing upon her chin she had fractured one of her jaw joints. Although the fracture had healed, it was alleged she could not open her jaw or eat normally and was seeking financial compensation. When I examined her, her limitation of opening was severe. I could see the muscles in her neck pulling hard to open the jaw. However, I also noticed her jaw did not deviate towards the fixed side as it normally would. I commiserated with her and sympathized with her many eating problems. After I had finished my examination, as I turned away, I said 'I forgot to examine your throat – say ahhhh!.' She opened her mouth wide and noised ahhhh. Our eyes met and she knew I knew. When I repeated the request she could not open her jaw one millimetre. We met again in the County Court of Haverfordwest but the presiding Judge, Michael Evans QC, was determined to savage the Highways Department and the plaintiff had the support of another consultant who believed her. Judge Evans found in her favour. There is an industry of litigation based upon spurious claims. If one adds to the cost of this, the enormous costs of the criminal compensation scheme and the succession of drunken grievous bodily harm cases appearing in every Crown Court, it is a huge wasted sum of money. I learned to rely on my findings not on what the plaintiff claimed. Many do not know what the oath means.

Limitation of jaw opening is potentially a serious problem if an anaesthetic is required or an acute throat infection develops, for access may be limited. A male in his twenties presented with an acute infection caused by impacted wisdom teeth. He could barely open his mouth. He had all the physical facial and cranial signs of Gargoylism, an inherited condition. Radiographic examination of his facial skeleton demonstrated that the cause of his acute problems was his wisdom teeth but the reason he could not open his jaws was the bilateral hugely enlarged coronoid processes of bone into which the temporal muscle is inserted. At the top of each process was a knob which impacted against the inside of the cheekbone as the jaw opened. To get to the wisdom teeth these processes had first to be sectioned. After a full discussion with my senior anaesthetist, we admitted the patient. The anaesthetist decided upon a blind intubation – a highly specialised technique which involves manipulating the anaesthetic tube down the nose and through the paralysed vocal cords. This was obviously difficult for it was some time before the patient was on the table.

Section of the enlarged processes was uncomplicated and allowed the jaws to be fully opened and the wisdom teeth to be surgically removed. I discussed the need for an elective tracheotomy but my anaesthetist advised this was not necessary after he examined the throat. For 36 hours the patient did well. He even took tea around the ward. My anaesthetic colleague and I were at a hospital dinner when I had a call to go down to the Infirmary immediately 15 minutes away. I found my houseman in a panic. Our patient had suddenly complained of breathing difficulties and had collapsed. We found him on his bed pulseless and without breathing. I immediately started to do a tracheotomy but could not find the trachea. I did find a thin vertical tube about one centimetre wide that I did not recognise. I tried to push and rotate the sharp ends of the scissors into it without success. This had to be his windpipe. I tried to push a needle into the pipe but the needle bent. By this time too much time had elapsed and we stopped all resuscitation. Post mortem examination demonstrated haemorrhagic blockage of the vocal cord area and an abnormal solid cartilaginous windpipe with thick walls and a narrow lumen. These abnormalities had not been described previously. I am not certain what would have been the long term result if we had done an elective tracheotomy at operation. We should have done one if we had known of this abnormality. The reconstruction of his trachea would have required techniques that I am not certain existed then.

There was yet another family tragedy to come. His first cousin, about the same age, also was a gargoyle or a mucopolysaccharidosis patient with limitation of jaw opening which he decided not to have corrected. He required an appendectomy after developing abdominal pain. Forewarned, the general surgeons thoroughly investigated him and he was found to have a similar abnormal trachea. Everything was prepared, including a planned post-operative admission to intensive care. Despite this, his airways obstructed post-operatively and attempts to relieve the obstruction failed. Medicine can be cruel to all concerned.

In the late summer of 1970 after finishing an afternoon outpatient clinic, I went to Cardiff Golf Club to play with a student, Mike James, who was much better at the game. As we waited to drive off I saw a young woman coming off the ninth green. She was in shorts, and had a good sun tan. 'Who is that?' I asked Mike. 'I think she works at the CRI. I'll find out.' He got her name and said she was a micro-biologist.

I rang her up at work, introduced myself and invited her to have dinner. I was to pick her up from her home and she arranged for her mother to vet me as I approached. If I failed, 'Jill has been delayed at work' was to be the excuse.

We had our meal without difficulty and three months later were engaged. We married in April 1971 and had two children in two years, Richard and Claire. Robert arrived seven years later when I was 46, the same age as my father when I was born. Robert was a 'mistake' we were delighted to make and we remain so.

15 Junior Trainees in Cardiff

In those days all consultants were backed up by a team of junior staff who assisted the consultant on the wards, clinics and operating theatres. In return, consultants taught their juniors the principles and practice of their discipline appropriate to their experience in post. consultants who enjoy teaching can be most influential whilst dogmatism and arrogance can be a turn off.

When I arrived in Cardiff, I was not considered suitable to become a clinical teacher by the Dean. However, the word got around that there was much to see and learn on my clinics and I found dental students turning up asking if they could join me. Before long too many became the problem. The students then asked if they could come over to theatre to watch and, again, we soon had to limit the number attending. The Dean must have learned of this activity for he requested that I be awarded an honorary clinical teacher contract by the University.

I expected these students to look and behave professionally. Those who came to the clinic scruffy were sent away to smarten up. I expected our teaching to be two way and questioned them on applied anatomy and physiology which they had covered in the second BDS course relating to the patient before them. Some students later claimed they were apprehensive of me but they still came to my clinics and operating theatre lists. Many years later some can repeat verbatim what they allege I said when they were students. I can't remember so I can't deny it. I cannot also deny that I am satisfied I made some impact.

From these interested dental students came the housemen – male and female who, not being medically qualified, found it was a big step to be first call in the A & E Department, resident in the Cardiff Royal Infirmary and required to clerk in all patients, elective and emergency. Their immediate training came from the registrar and senior registrar, whilst I often supervised their elementary work in theatre. Several of these juniors went on to make a career in the discipline and to qualify in Medicine – a considerable sacrifice for them financially. In 2008 I was invited to attend the Annual Conference of the British Association of Oral and Maxillofacial Surgeons (BAOMS) held in Cardiff and chaired by David Patten from Swansea. I was delighted and amazed by the number of my juniors and past students who were now consultants. I felt like Mr. Chips. Before I arrived in Cardiff, no senior registrar had achieved a consultant post. After I arrived they all did. Not all senior registrars were medically qualified but I did not differentiate between what I expected them to do. Whilst it is true only one of the singly qualified senior registrars has had an exceptional career, Adrian Sugar, not all of those doubly qualified had either. I am sure all did the job to the best of their ability without establishing a national reputation. However, several have which gives me much pleasure. Only two (both doubly qualified) were unsuitable for surgical training and one I persuaded to take up another discipline in which he retired a Professor. The other was an academic oral surgeon. His clinical care of patients was such that I saw the Dean and told him I would involve the General Medical Council if he was not stopped. He was transferred to another Teaching Hospital. Another nail in my academic coffin!

Without doubt the acquisition of a medical qualification and training enabled oral surgery to move into Maxillofacial surgery and to throw off the yoke of plastic surgery. The European Medical Directives declared the discipline a medical mono-speciality requiring qualifications in both Medicine and Dentistry. One hoped to attract doubly qualified candidates to Wales but not everybody found Wales or the Welsh language attractive, even those Welsh born. There was a significant number of registrar and senior registrars who were singly qualified. It was not easy to make up a short list with suitably qualified candidates and some doubly qualified registrars lacked charisma. An additional problem I faced in Cardiff was that the new Dean of the Dental School (who replaced Professor Cooke), Professor Norman Robertson, did not favour any candidate I supported and the school representative, on an appointment committee, followed his lead. I supported the best candidate at appointment committees. I was angered therefore when a retired colleague from Sussex told me, and presumably others, that it was well known that I favoured singly qualified candidates so that I could shine in their shadow. The only time that I did favour a singly qualified candidate was Adrian Sugar at Chepstow. His subsequent career and his international reputation has been significant. The BAOMS has just awarded him the Downs Surgical medal for 2013. The doubly qualified candidate favoured by the plastic surgeons sadly did not prosper and died prematurely after a peripatetic career.

One pleasing coincidence is that my daughter Claire, a rhinologist and skull base surgeon at Guy's, occasionally operates with Rob Bentley, a Maxillofacial surgeon at King's; he was one of my juniors who went on to read Medicine. He heads emergency care at King's and is seen frequently on TV.

My relationship with the Dean, Professor Cooke, and his colleagues remained wary. Three years after my appointment I dropped two sessions to become part-time and start a private consultant practice. The Dean told me that I would never be heard of again and would never get a Distinction Award. He was wrong on both counts. My career became national and international as the spectrum of my work continued to expand. To my surprise, Professor Miller, the Vice Dean twice suggested to me that I take an interest in applying for the Chair of Oral Surgery, obviously with the agreement of Professor Cooke. Each time, after talking the matter over with my wife Jill, I decided that I could not work in the same team as Cooke. Also I was not attracted to the prospect of lecturing, teaching and examining undergraduates. Had I accepted, my subsequent career would have been very different.

16 The Early Days of my Involvement in Medical Politics

A few years after coming to Cardiff I was elected Secretary and then Chairman of the Dental Staff Sub-Committee, a sub-committee of the main Medical Staff Committee of South Glamorgan. As such, I had a seat on the Committee which was elected by the Medical Board, composed of all consultants employed by the South Glamorgan Health Authority. I was elected to the Welsh Consultants Committee and from that Committee I was elected to the Central Committee for Hospital Medical Services. John Chawner, a North-Walian Obstetric & Gynae. Consultant, and I replaced two aged and silent consultants from Wales. It was not long before we were elected to the General Purposes & Negotiating committee of the Central Committee for Hospital Medical Services (CCHMS). Those sub-committees took us onto the British Medical Association (BMA) Council and the Joint Consultants Committee. In a short time we had become influential but, whereas John supported the BMA line, I often found myself at variance from the leadership of the BMA, particularly Tony Grabham – later knighted – the Chairman of the Council.

A coterie of consultants and junior doctors believed that the Government should give the necessary money to the NHS and leave the doctors to decide how it should be spent. My view was that if the NHS was to be successful, the professions had to stop being profligate with money, to spend it wisely on evidence-based clinical services, to stop over investigating and over prescribing and finally, to become involved in the management of the NHS as the existing administration was too pathetic to succeed. I spoke against the Chairman of Councils' demand for more money at the Newcastle Conference and at another suggested that the NHS staff were more comfortable than the patients. Three Prime Minister's questions were put to Mrs. Thatcher as a result of these and other press coverage which, along with a few letters in the broad sheets, may have resulted in an invitation to be in 'Who's Who' in 1994. At least that is my belief but nobody really knows how you get into it.

In 1980 I had become Chairman of the Medical Staff Committee of South Glamorgan and had a seat on the Area Team of management. One of many reorganisations of the NHS had resulted in the introduction of line management for each professional group with no embracing general management. The Area Team which consisted of the Administrator, Finance Officer, Medical Officer, Chief Nurse and Engineer/Architect rotated the Chairmanship every three months. No major decision was ever taken and the weekly meetings were a huge time waste. Instead of managing the financial situation, they imposed financial cuts so that operations were cancelled, admissions reduced, waiting lists increased, windows not cleaned and grass not cut. Morale plummeted and conditions deteriorated. I learned of the abuse of the NHS by several consultants; my belief grew that unless the consultants became actively involved in management and used their brains and leadership, the NHS would collapse. We had endured the horror of the winter of discontent in 1973 when we had to get approval from shop stewards to admit patients for surgery and we had seen Jim Callaghan replaced by Mrs. Thatcher. She asked the chief executive of Sainsbury to carry out a review of NHS Management. The Griffiths Enquiry took evidence from many sources, including the BMA, through which I participated in the in house campaign to get doctors involved. The CCHMS finally agreed to recommend this to Griffiths and he included doctors amongst those who could apply to be a general manager of health units. Tony Grabham remained opposed to the principle to the bitter end.

Activity within the London BMA committees necessitated early morning train journeys from Cardiff. Experience had taught me to observe a medical emergency and determine if it was likely I could help before announcing I was a doctor. Towards the end of a winter journey to London the guard called for medical assistance over the loud speaker. I did not react expecting several doctors to volunteer. A repeat call got me out of my seat to make my way to the named carriage. I entered it to see the guard standing beside four people sitting with a table between them. A young lady was sitting next to the window with a neighbours head resting on her shoulder. She looked scarred stiff and he looked dead. 'How long has he been like this?' I asked. 'Twenty minutes', was the reply. I confirmed he was dead and looked around for assistance. I asked three nearby males to help me lift him from his seat. The passenger was wearing an overcoat and it was difficult to get a grip of him. I said - on the count of three we would lift him up and outwards. On the number three we all lifted together and his overcoat came up leaving him behind at the bottom of the table. It would have been a good trick in other circumstances.

We got him out of the carriage and laid him on the floor besides the toilet doors. I covered him up with his overcoat. Just then a breathless young man arrived and announced he was a medical student. I told him the patient was dead and had been for at least 20 minutes. 'We must do cardiac massage for him' he replied. 'Good', I said. 'we've just passed Reading and you must keep it up until we get to Paddington'. He decided not to start. Weeks later I got a letter from British Rail thanking me for going to the assistance of a 'passenger taken ill on the train'. 'Good heavens', I thought, 'did he live?'

17 Overseas Lecture Tours - USA, India, South Africa and Hong Kong.

Each year, Khursheed Moos invited me to participate in his oral and maxillofacial surgery course at Canniesburn Hospital, at Glasgow. The attendees were a mixture of home-grown and overseas students, mostly registrars, but some seniors came, mainly from overseas. One such was Athol Frew, who headed the service in Oklahoma City. He invited me to go over to his centre to lecture and teach his residents for a week. He said he would have arranged other visits by the time I arrived. The medical centre in Oklahoma at that time was newly built and expanding - the facilities and equipment mind boggling. However, oral surgery was essentially 'office-based' but the service included facial trauma. No one was medically qualified.

My memory of this visit was of working hard and lecturing all the first day. When we finished, Athol took me to a nearby burger restaurant where I ordered my burger. What arrived was a quadruple deck of meat and salads. I did not know how to eat such a bulk of food, so I picked up my knife and fork and made a start. Across the restaurant were four males at a table wearing cowboy hats – one called out 'God Damn! There's a man eating a hamburger with a knife and fork.' So started a long evening, assisted by repeated Budweisers and their listening to my accent in amazement.

Athol had arranged for me to go to Houston and decided to drive me down – a trip of about 1,000 miles, if my memory is correct. He was addicted to cigarettes and to Californian Chablis, which he imbibed all the way down from large pump thermos flasks. As we entered Texas he called on a wartime friend. I was introduced as coming from Cardiff, England, which I corrected to Wales. Our host then said I would never have heard of Maenclochog, emphasising the three syllables. 'I was there in the war,' he said. 'You must have been in the tanks training at Rosebush,' I replied. 'God damn – this man knows Rosebush.' To meet somebody in Texas who knew two small villages on the Preseli hills in North Pembrokeshire was a surprise. In Houston I stayed with an ex-American Air Force Dental Officer I had met in our conferences in the UK. He lived in luxury around a golf course. On a brilliant sunny day his wife put the washing into a drying machine. I asked why she didn't hang the clothes outside to dry. She thought that a strange idea. I was offended by the excessive use of energy wherever I went.

My second US trip was a lecture tour, organised by Roger Gerry, an anglophile, and it covered about a dozen or more teaching centres. My itinerary was to travel by plane to a centre, wine and dine that evening, next day attend clinics or view operations then small group teaching and discussion, third day eight hours of lecturing then off to the next place. It was exhausting in the extreme, worsened by jetlag and the fact that my mother died the weekend before the trip started and I had not attended her funeral. These lectures were attended by hundreds of clinicians who had cancelled their patients and clinics to attend. I rationalised that my mother would have wished me to go ahead, but to this day I regret I was not there for her cremation. The equipment of all the hospitals was breathtaking, as were the houses of my hosts but it seemed to me they were not any happier than us and I did not respond positively to two feelers put to me to stay. In one teaching centre I found the technicians copying my slides to add to their chief's collection. I was not amused.

Soon before I was to fly from Oklahoma City to Houston my hosts lunched me at the Oil Man's Club. I was then poured onto the aircraft, fastened my seat belt and went to sleep with the sun streaming through the window.

Sometime later I came round realising that all was not well. I was soaked in sweat and found it difficult to see or think. I became aware I was fainting with a low blood pressure as a result of a full stomach, alcohol and over-heating. I had to lie flat. Before standing I had to get my pressure up so I started isometric exercises of all limbs. As I regained the ability to focus I stood up and reached the aisle. Feeling OK I went aft and lay on the carpet outside the toilets and galley. I expected a flight attendant to enquire how I was but instead everybody stepped over me without comment. When I had recovered I sat up, whereupon an attendant asked me if I needed a doctor! There's none so blind as those who don't wish to see; I could have been dead.

India was a shock to my system. I did two visits. The first, at the behest of the British Council, was to teach at the King George V Hospital and Dental School in Lucknow. The attendees were oral surgeons of varying degrees of experience from around India. They were a most appreciative group but I think my subject matter may have been beyond the facilities or equipment to which they had access. However, we did start an exchange of juniors between Cardiff and Lucknow which was valuable to both sides. It did set them a target to aspire to. It was the poverty that struck me most forcibly. Nothing was thrown away until it had been recycled several times. The average inhabitant lived in depressing accommodation. Road sense was non-existent, horns were sounded continually and cows wandered all over the roads. The air was heavy with smoke and the smell of faeces and there was hardly a second that did not interest me. I was to sleep in an old palace in a bedroom the size of an aircraft hangar.

Lucknow

Without a mosquito net I could hear the mosquitoes start their attacking run at me from afar and could not sleep. I demanded new accommodation and was put in a University hostel with modern accommodation and a mosquito net. I slept.

I was asked to operate upon a temporo mandibular joint to which I agreed but when I saw the patient who had a swelling near the joint, I noticed he also had facial weakness so I said this was probably a salivary malignancy. Oh well please do that. As there was only one morning left of my stay, I agreed without working up the investigations. In theatre, as the patient was being anaesthetised, I scrubbed and powdered my hands as we did 20 years ago and then picked up a theatre gown which was full of holes and so was the next. I found one with smaller holes and then put on my gloves. As I pulled up the cuff it came away. The gloves were old and boiled too often. I was too used to disposable gloves in the UK. As I dissected the parotid gland tumour away, the patient started to move. The anaesthetist said she was running out of Trilene and could I hurry up. I am a relatively quick surgeon but was not quick enough for Lucknow. It was all a sobering experience for me, particularly as it was difficult to find a bottle of cold beer.

After Lucknow, I visited several centres along the Ganges river and then Madras and Bangalore. I doubted that I would be able to eat their curries but I was surprised to be told that only in the UK are the curries hot. In Cawnpore I saw patients lying exposed on their beds whilst their relatives fed them after cooking the food in pots on wood fires in the courtyard. There were virtually no nurses and many patients came in from the country with sores or cancers infested with maggots. I was shown a little girl with a swollen face and saw that her upper jaw and soft tissues below the eye were full of them. Turpentine was the cure I was told. In Calcutta there was a period of student unrest and they were refusing to sit exams. I met a Professor of Pathology who burst into tears as he told me there was a minimum percentage of 'untouchable' medical students who had to pass their finals whether they were suitable or not.

On my return I wrote to the GMC telling them what I had seen and heard. They replied their inspectors had given glowing reports on these same institutions.

On my second visit to Lucknow, ostensibly to give the Chowla Oration, I saw a number of UK donated mobile clinics standing idle outside of the hospital for want of spare parts. Just as I started the Oration in front of an invited audience of dignitaries, there was a bang and electricity failed. I had to give my talk without slides and in semi-darkness. Hardly satisfactory.

My wife came with me and we had a hair raising drive to Khajuraho where the uncovered ancient temples demonstrated thousands of stone carvings which showed that was nothing new today with sex with humans or animals. The Taj Mahal , truly a wonder of the world – quite breathtaking. No photograph can catch the atmosphere and its beauty.

We were talking quite normally to another couple when Jill said she felt ill. Within minutes she was acutely unwell with diarrhoea and vomiting. She had eaten a salad. 48 hours later all was well. Beware of uncooked food.

Professor Chowla had been the Dean of the Dental School on my first visit. He was a scholarly, kind individual who arranged for me to go to a meeting of the Indian surgeons at Patna to lecture. On the way we stopped off to visit Varanasi and the holy Ganges, where people bathed in water full of excrement and a few corpses. One passed us as we boated up river with a crow eating the exposed flesh. We should have been in Patna by then but Chowla was unconcerned. We arrived at the meeting to find an actual fight going on on the platform. My enquires elicited that the officers of the Association were attacking the State Minister of Health. I cannot remember if I gave the lecture but nobody worried that I was 24 hours late!

The British Council arranged for me to visit the South African Universities during the time of apartheid. Although the whites prospered, it was easy to believe time was standing still there in their isolation and I did not enjoy this visit that much. I found some Afrikaners difficult to like. The country, however, was wonderful. I saw enough machete wounds to last me a lifetime and patients lying under, as well as on, the beds in Baragwaneth Hospital outside of Jo'burg. I then realised what a busy hospital really was. The Association of Maxillofacial & Oral Surgery of South Africa made me an Honorary Life Member which was much appreciated.

In 1992 Professor Hank Tideman asked me to be an examiner in Hong Kong which I did for three years. You cannot mix with the Chinese without becoming aware of their industry and endeavour. My visits in February were always busy, enjoyable and I gorged on delicious Chinese cuisine. I took the opportunity to get shirts, shoes and a suit made each time I went which was usually around the Chinese New Year. A friend asked me to buy his wife a watch and I had thought of buying a cheap valise in which to carry the extra clothes home. I went into a store which I learned later was the Harrods of Hong Kong and bought a watch in the 50% off sale. Nearby I saw suit carriers on a rack and one which caught my eye was made of leather. I mentally converted the cost from HK dollars and it came out just over £50 which was about £40 more than I intended to spend. I was impressed by it so I bought it. As I checked in for my flight home I threw my case and the suit carrier onto the luggage train for transition to the hold. When I got home my wife commented upon the carrier and the softness of the leather. 'It should be' I said, 'at half price it was still over £50.' 'Well,' she said, 'small handbags of that make cost more.' A month later my card print-out showed the price of the carrier was £550 and a letter to the store confirmed that before the sale the bag had been priced at £1,100. I had no idea a suitcase could cost that much. So much for my mental arithmetic for the conversion of foreign currency! Needless to say, I took more care of it afterwards.

I made many visits to European countries and established a network of colleagues in those countries.

18 Saudi Arabia - Local and Long Term Problems

Bill Heald had been asked by Whittaker International, an American firm, to set up a 'Physician Evaluation Board' (PEB), to check out the suitability of medical and dental staff applying to work in their hospitals in Saudi which cared for members of the Royal Family, the National Guard and their families. Bill asked me if I would look after the dental and maxillofacial component and I willingly agreed. Most of the work involved reviewing applications in the UK, but once a year it was necessary to visit the hospitals to review the work done, the facilities and equipment. The company headquarters were in Riyadh but the four other hospitals were scattered around Saudi. Whilst the majority of the senior staff were European and mainly British, there were also several Asians, mainly Indian. The tax-free salaries then were a major attraction and most of the UK medical staff had either had trouble getting a senior UK post, money or divorce problems. For the Asians who were paid less than the Brits and Americans for doing the same work, it was a major opportunity for them to be well paid to work in hospitals with excellent facilities. The function of the PEB was to ensure these staff were all trained to do the job required of them.

A major problem for expat senior staff was that Saudi law demanded that a Saudi was the titular head. This resulted in every senior clinical or lay departmental head being responsible to a local who could be good but generally was not. Some Saudi departmental heads had spent some time in the UK or USA, ostensibly training, but many seemed to have trained in night clubs rather than hospitals. The 'good ones' kept out of the way, taking the money but not the work, but we heard many complaints of the quality of work done by those who actually attempted to manage. Arrogance usually accompanied uselessness so that working in such a department could be difficult. One compensation for this was the wonderful expensive equipment found everywhere, but particularly in Jeddah where the Royal Family, of which there were hundreds, were cared for.

At each hospital we visited and lectured we met the expat staff socially in their exclusive living compounds. With their clubs, sports facilities, swimming pools (no mixed bathing), and home brewed beer and wine, they had a pleasant if difficult life, particularly if female. Many nurses told us of sexual advances and abuse from Saudi males and they were not able to drive a motorcar. However, overseas leave was generous and it was common for staff to make sufficient money to return to their own countries after 5 to 10 years.

I cannot remember from where, but we went in a Land Rover into the desert and were shown the original railway line built by the Turks in World War I and attacked by Lawrence and his Arab armies. Railway engines and trucks lay in the same place where they had been blown up virtually free of rust. I wanted to know why the railway lines had been taken up and piled in heaps; it was to stop invading armies using the railway. We also found a pile of volcanic rocks on which there are Stone Age carvings of African bush animals of all types. This whole area of sand and rocky desert must have been covered in bush with a climate that fed plants and the animals. The local population was then African and not Arab.

My trips to Saudi were terminated when Whittaker International lost the contract to manage the National Guard Hospitals but a Saudi connection was reborn in 1986 when I was the General Manager of the University Hospital in Wales in Cardiff. One day I had a surprise telephone call. Was I interested in going to a hospital in Saudi Arabia to ascertain why it was always in difficulty? If so, would I like to go to the Rome Hilton to meet Prince Feisal bin Abdulla bin Mohammed. So off I went to Rome and was given a most luxurious room. I then met the Prince who introduced me to his wife and children, all delightful and wearing western dress. I listened to him recounting that this hospital seemed incapable of staying within its budget – money seemingly disappeared! Then he took me shopping and presented me with a beautiful silk tie that is still in use. That night I joined the family for a meal in a restaurant and later I went to sleep wondering if I was flying on a magic carpet. The Prince had agreed I would take a small team, so I recruited our accountant and personnel officer and we all took annual leave for one week. We flew Saudi Airlines first class in a jumbo to Riyadh and were taken to our accommodation in an air conditioned hotel. The next day we met the hospital management, the headman being a minor prince. I spent the day meeting the medical staff whilst my colleagues delved into their areas of expertise. By the end of day two it was clear that corruption at all levels of the Saudi management was the main culprit. Saudiisation had been fully implemented and each department had its expat head that was responsible to the Saudi head. The expat managers appeared to be helpless in the circumstances. Mike Lewis, at our briefing meeting, gave one example of the many he had uncovered by going over the books. A pair of surgical boots costing the hospital say £3.05p, actually cost the hospital £35 by the time the bill was paid – each department the boots passed through added 10-20% handling charges for the 'back pocket'. All the heads and the top prince were on the take.

As we walked into the hospital one morning, a European brushed past me and I felt something pushed into my jacket pocket. I turned around to see the male person hurrying away. I found a sealed envelope in my pocket – 'Do not open in public' it said. It burned a hole in my pocket all day but back in my hotel bedroom that evening, I sat down to read its contents. The head store man, a Brit, had been sentenced to 60 lashes with a cane. His crime – he had put his feet up on his desktop facing his Saudi workers and by doing so he had insulted Allah and them. My correspondent alleged the British management were doing nothing to help him and he felt isolated, neglected and very apprehensive of the forthcoming beating. Could I help him? Next day I spoke to the senior British manager and asked what was going on. I was told that the head of stores had come to the conclusion his Saudi workers were stealing supplies from the stores and that he had accused them. They responded that he had insulted them by this and by putting his feet on the desk and showing them the soles of his shoes. The religious police had arrested him and he was to be lashed. However, the British managers had no doubt that in due course their considerable efforts would result in the sentence being either cancelled or reduced in some way. I was assured all would be well.

After we returned home we prepared a report on our several findings of malfunction and corruption and after it was finished I realised I did not know where to send it. I had no address of the prince – I could not send it to the hospital and I finally addressed it to the Prince c/o the Saudi Embassy. I did not receive any acknowledgement of its receipt and I later met a member of its staff who said that nothing had changed. Perhaps the prince merely wished to know how much was being taken.

A year or more later when I went to my hospital office in Cardiff, I found a reporter waiting to see me. He had learned that I knew about a Brit who was about to be lashed in Saudi. It took me a while to recall the person. A small report appeared in a broadsheet and suddenly I was in receipt of calls from all over, including London Radio. 'Was it not uncivilised to give a man 60 lashes?' I was asked. 'Well yes, it would be,' I replied, 'but you have to remember that the beater has a copy of the Koran under his armpit and that must reduce the force of the blow. It must be unpleasant but it may not be as bad as it sounds.' I answered the questions carefully for the prince had asked me whether I would wish to visit the hospital regularly to check upon progress. I had agreed for I knew it would be a pension booster. That evening I listened to Classic Radio news and they played my interview. The question about being uncivilised was followed by my reply, 'Yes'. I had fallen for a lousy trick; they had edited out my qualification about holding the Koran. It was the old problem of a recorded answer which the editor could edit as he wished. It was a lesson learned the hard way. The next day I had a call from the Saudi Embassy. 'Had I called the punishment uncivilised?' I don't believe they were interested in my side of the story and that was the end of my Saudi experience. I smile when I read about the bribery allegations and the UK arms industry. That is the only way to get business in Saudi Arabia. Everybody there is on the take. The PEB made one visit to Kuwait where we had tea with the Emir. The atmosphere in Kuwait was quite different.

19 President of British Association of Oral and Maxillofacial Surgeons

Before World War II selected university trained dentists looked after the dental needs of in-patients. These visiting professionals would leave their dental practices to extract teeth from medically compromised patients. Post extraction haemorrhage or dental/facial pain in an in-patient could also result in a call. Some may have assisted their surgeons with jaw fractures helped by Sir William Kelsey Fry's book which was based upon his own World War 1 experience. World War II expanded the horizons and experience of those dental officers who were involved in the treatment of facial injury. Some dental officers gave the general anaesthetics and were involved in the care of the injured in the forward hospitals. These dental officers brought home with them clinical confidence and experience.

With the start of the NHS a number of dentists were given consultant contracts. Not all of them had the skills and confidence to throw off the yoke of general, ENT, orthopaedic or plastic surgery. The NHS established a training pathway for dental surgeons and senior registrar training posts were established. Some were sited in dental teaching hospitals from which the trainee gained limited experience. Other senior registrars were sited in regional plastic and jaw units where they were usually dominated by the medical surgeons.

Tom Battersby's skills and personality enabled him to develop a major service which broke away from plastic surgery control; consultants like him were few. He was helped in this by possessing the diploma of Fellowship in Dental Surgery of the Royal College of Surgeons (FDSRCS), developed in the 1950s to raise the standards and knowledge of potential dental specialists. It was a two part exam based upon the Fellowship of the Royal College of Surgeons (FRCS). The FDSRCS was the passport to a consultant post.

An increasing number of those dentally qualified also qualified in medicine. Perhaps they followed the example of our continental cousins who qualified first in medicine and then took dentistry as a medical speciality. Increasingly, adverts for Consultant Oral Surgeons required a dental qualification, an FDS and a medical qualification! How was I to know I would soon apply for a registrar's post with Norman Rowe, the author of the advertisement. At the end of this post I became a medical student!

Several of those who qualified in medicine did not do house jobs or register as medical practitioners. I could not see the point of this for there

As President

is no substitute for experiencing medicine or surgery on a sick or dying patient in the middle of the night. Of those who gained the medical qualification simply as a 'rubber stamp' few went on to gain a good surgical reputation.

There was a wide spectrum of surgical skill and practice in oral surgery in the 1960s. Relatively few pushed out the boundaries and attempted to establish the independence of the discipline. I was deeply frustrated by two senior consultants who both had the general surgery FRCS but who limited their surgical practice to routine oral surgery and even dentistry. That didn't stop some from inferring they were doing great things. The phrase 'I prefer to do it this way' heard in bars or the Oral Surgery Club really meant for some 'I prefer somebody else to do it this way while I hold the retractor'. Many of these people were in influential posts with junior staff to train and it was several years before the Royal College of Surgeons and the British Association of Oral and Maxillofacial Surgeons put that right. My opinions about this became known and I was blackballed from the Oral Surgery Club by David Downton, a friend of Geoffrey Howe.

The establishment of the FRCS in maxillo-facial surgery by the Royal College of Surgeons of Edinburgh in the 1980s was a trump card in gaining acceptance as a recognised surgical discipline. The speciality owed much to the efforts of Laurie Finch, John Gould and Khursheed Moos, who persuaded the College Council of the merits of the case. This fellowship was followed by inter-collegiate fellowship. Initially, doubly qualified consultants could complete a short course to enable them to be examined. I regret now that I did not do this but I was then the general manager of the University Hospital of Wales and my priorities were not clinical.

I am full of admiration for the stamina and success of my successors in our speciality. They have a very long period of training and multiple exams and their successors have the worry of how to finance their undergraduate training. I hold in high esteem my predecessors who made the break-through in our battle for clinical independence. Maxillofacial surgery is truly now a respected surgical discipline. The connection to dentistry and the faculties of the Royal Colleges grows more tenuous. However as the speciality becomes increasingly surgical and hospital orientated we should be aware that our patients benefit from a service which combines medicine with dentistry. We should continue to provide oral surgery which is essential for training junior staff.

The British Association of Oral and Maxillofacial Surgeons played a crucial role in the development of the discipline, both in the UK and internationally, through its Journal and bi-annual conferences. It was now possible to listen to and read papers detailing developments and know who was making them. I was first elected to Council, became Treasurer and finally President in 1993. The principal task of the President was the spring conference. The President is responsible for the local organisation of the conference, with the central secretariat doing much of the routine work. I set up a local committee of colleagues who included Michael Hill. He was a tower of organisational skills. The meeting was a success held in the City Hall, Cardiff. The Llanelli Male Voice Choir standing on the marble staircase at the end of the entrance hall raised the hair on our necks. The meeting set two records - one, the amount of money raised for our Association, a charity, and two, the lateness of the hour of the finish of the dinner. After logistical problems delayed the start I aggravated the problem by giving my prepared speech to take advantage of the presence of a government minister. I should have ditched it completely.

My wife ran the accompanying person's programme, including its organisation, and visit to Big Pit at Blaenavon. Her mother died that same morning but Jill carried on with great courage without the ladies realising what had happened. We both lost our mothers at most inconvenient times.

I gained much satisfaction from my Presidency and being adding to an illustrious list. My memory tells me that I was present in the gentleman's toilet at the College, attending a meeting of the European Association, when John Hovell, of St Thomas's, and Norman Rowe, of Roehampton, standing side by side, spoke together about forming the British Association. I was there at the beginning!

20 A Change of Job - General Manager, University Hospital of Wales

Anybody reading the description of my patients' problems might believe my surgery was full of crises. In reality the vast majority of patients' surgery was routine and successful, although often complicated and time consuming. Much of what I did I actually enjoyed, such as salivary gland and cancer surgery but though I enjoyed sectioning the facial skeleton into several pieces, its reconstruction with shaped bone grafts, plates and screws was time consuming, boring and left me worn out. The needs of senior registrars pushed me to use all of the latest techniques and I began to dislike extra-long operating lists. I was 53, getting out of my comfort zone and I could see what was going to be my life until I retired. I was ready for a change in 1985. The advertisement for the General Management posts of the South Glamorgan Health Units attracted my attention. Unit 2 was to be the University Hospital, the Dental Hospital and Ely Children's Hospital. It was to be the largest Unit in Wales, with a budget then of over £64M. Ignorance prevented me from understanding what a huge task this would be, particularly for somebody who had not been in management. I applied for Unit 2, not believing I had a chance of success.

The newly appointed District General Manager (DGM), Gordon Harrhy, asked to see me. He wondered if I would be interested in one of the other Units, but I replied that if I did not get Unit 2, I would rather remain a clinician. Even if appointed I intimated that I wished to maintain the limited number of three clinical sessions permitted. I needed to remain on the Distinction Award ladder, open only to those who did clinical work. The DGM said that if appointed I would be given a six week period of introduction and training. I learned that I was shortlisted for Unit 2 and that my principle opposition was Alan Trew, then the acting general manager of the University Hospital of Wales (UHW). I did not expect to get the job.

The interview panel consisted of the new Chairman, Alan Jones, a solicitor and unsuccessful Conservative parliamentary candidate; the DGM of South Glamorgan; the DGM of Singleton Hospital, Swansea, John Button, and a non-executive member of the Authority. I cannot now remember the questions, apart from what would I do first if appointed. Amongst other things I said because I believed people worked better in a good environment I would get the windows cleaned for the first time in twelve years and the grass cut. I would then get to know, in detail, the empire and the people for which I was responsible. The next day, a Friday, I was called to see Gordon Harrhy who told me I was to be the UGM of

As manager of the University Hospital of Wales ©Media Wales

Unit 2 and that I would start on the next Monday morning. No six week introduction for me – I was to start immediately. I accepted, but insisted I would require training, to which he agreed.

I have often wondered why the panel took such a risk in appointing me. I am quite sure that if a quality career manager had applied, he or she would have got it. There were no outside applicants. Perhaps they did not wish to risk their future career where two or three had failed before? Whatever the reason, the biggest job in Wales, at that time, went to somebody sublimely ignorant of what was entailed and least prepared for what was to come.

That Monday morning I sat down behind the desk in my new office. 'Bloody Hell' I thought, 'what have I done?' I had taken over the management of three hospitals. Of these the UHW was the most complex with 850 beds, 125 consultants, 850 nurses, working in tandem with the medical school and clinical academia. The hospital had a long history of running out of money in the winter and long term cost reductions. The windows, of which there were many, had not been cleaned for 12 years and the grass on site was cut once a year, if that. The wards were dirty. I had the simplistic view that if the workplace environment was neglected, the quality of work would match it and vice versa. I had little knowledge of the theory of management, but I did have clinical logic and common sense. As a child I had gone with my father who was the general manager of Sunderland Corporation Transport on his afternoon visits to the tram and bus depots. He would talk to the fitters, blacksmiths and managers about work problems and their families whilst I watched them working. He knew all of their names and I remembered this as I sat behind the desk. I would go 'walkabouts'.

I called in the senior management staff who were on temporary contracts and the senior nurse, one by one, to introduce myself. There was no accountant for he only attended one afternoon a month! The deputy hospital administrator, who was seconded from District, was welcoming but the personnel manager was very frosty. I gained the immediate impression she viewed me as an imposter. Having visited the management staff in adjacent offices to say hello, I went on the first of my walkabouts. I was the first and probably the last senior manager to repeatedly visit the kitchens, mortuary, records, storerooms and all the clinical areas. It took several days to converse with the staff, but when I had finished I had a clearer idea of my task.

I met the DGM, who was then planning the management structure for each Unit, to request an immediate transfer of a full-time accountant to start identifying where and how much money was being spent. There was no detailed financial or statistical information available for any of the hospitals or the clinical services; staff numbers were vague and management control non-existent. The administration was the servant of the clinicians who did what they wanted, when and how they wished. I was told I would have to wait for a full-time accountant. It was now perfectly clear why the hospital was repeatedly overspent. All Unit General Managers (UGM) were to remain responsible and accountable to the DGM. Management changes and any capital expenditure over a limit had to have his approval. This was a continual problem for me.

I called the senior unit management together and told them I did not wish to hear the terms 'Administrator' or 'administration' used again. They were to manage, take their own decisions, manage their risks and involve me only if they were in trouble. People had to do the jobs they held and were paid for. At weekly senior team meetings, each department head would keep me aware of the problems and successes. When we received our management structure from District they could apply for their substantive posts in open competition. The Assistant General Manager would immediately find out why the place was dirty and get quotations for window cleaning and grass cutting. With that, I set off to the NHS Management College in Harrogate. My five days there gave me a very good idea why NHS management was incompetent. I was depressed by the poverty of the instruction. There was a lot of management speak but nobody seemed to know how to manage anything. When I returned I found that the DGM's management structure had been published and was identical for each of the 5 Units, despite their different sizes and complexities. Not for the last time I wondered if the DGM wished me to succeed. He had never managed a hospital and did not realise how much extra work was necessary to manage my three hospitals and pull them into shape.

We had failed to get a full-time accountant, although we did achieve an increase of his hours. Every conversation I had with Mike Lewis (the accountant) depressed me as he recounted how little we knew of what went on or how we could control expenditure. There was a minimum of information about bed occupancy, usage or clinical activity. Clinicians (like me) did what they wanted, when they wanted. Where and upon what money was spent was unknown; the management simply paid the bills until money ran out when elective surgery would be limited and outpatient services cancelled. I already had much respect for Mike Lewis and told him that somehow we had to control our expenditure. We agreed that a full-time financial team was essential immediately, for which I pressed the DGM and District Finance Officer. We finally got Mike plus two full-time assistants and purchased a desk computer for them. In 1985 we were at last on our way into modern accounting systems.

An early promulgation from me was that the management would no longer pay for any equipment or clinical service for which we had not previously agreed and budgeted. Consultants and academics had been in the habit of viewing new equipment at conferences which the manufacturers would encourage them to borrow for a trial period. Later the hospital management would be presented with a large bill, generally after twelve months of trialling and service development. Finding the money was management's problem, not the clinician's. This unplanned expenditure could involve staff as well as equipment. My consultant colleagues and the professors who paid little attention to my decision learned the hard way that I meant what I said. Despite their pleas, we refused to pay; equipment was returned or money found elsewhere. 'Borrowing' soon stopped. We had to have financial discipline.

I set up the Unit Management Team immediately. The medical voice, Dr. Ralph Vaughan, a consultant anaesthetist and the Chairman of the UHW Medical Staff Committee, put the medical view without fear or favour; the Chief Nurse was Annette Watkins, who had received her basic training in Cardiff Royal Infirmary and had become the Nurse Director of the Salford Health Authority (her husband's premature death had caused her to take the UHW post, a demotion, in order to come back to Wales). She was not office-bound like so many NHS senior managers. Her face was familiar on the wards, clinics and operating theatres; she put the nursing view strongly. 850 nurses were a good source of information and Annette was invaluable for reporting any unplanned developments and consultant misbehaviour. Clinicians repeatedly complained about nursing shortages, yet we were fully established. Maternity leave absence was inevitable but this was aggravated by considerable long term sick leave for GPs, not only over-prescribed drugs but also sick notes. I asked Mrs. Watkins to review all such cases and develop a scheme with our occupational health doctors, for better supervision, particularly as increased sickness seemed to coincide with the school holidays. I also requested her to collect information on bed occupancy, usage, blocking and fiddles used by clinicians and ward sisters to stop 'their' beds being used for emergency admissions by other disciplines.

It was not long before evidence accumulated of inappropriate bed allocations and misuse of nurses by clinicians. Principally to save money, we took one ward at a time out of commission in order to carry out essential refurbishment and redecoration. These wards had been in use for fourteen years without piped oxygen or suction and limited communication equipment. The ward nurses were reallocated to where there were actual shortages. With better information, I ordered changes to bed allocations, e.g. fifteen beds or half a ward were removed from the ophthalmologists who had a 50% bed occupancy and refused to consider cataract surgery as a day case, which was normal on medical charity ships off the African coast. The psychiatry ward was supposed to be used for acute admissions; however, most patients had been there for months and a few over a year. Some ward sisters failed to report the empty beds on their wards. The provision of another computer and twice daily visual checks by senior nurse management stopped these abuses. Consultants considered the ward beds theirs and I had to remind them time and time again that everything belonged to the NHS. The Professor of Haematology repeatedly complained about inadequate nursing numbers on his ward. I requested an in-depth assessment of what was going on. The Nurse Director told me that the ward nurses were devoting a considerable time to work that should be done by his laboratory technicians. I had already learned that the Professor was using twelve NHS senior scientific officers paid for from my budget for full-time research. He had several times got equipment and staff from the Welsh Office which should have been labour saving. I issued instructions that nurses would immediately stop work not considered to be within their remit by nurse managers. I did not wait long for the result. The Professor burst into my office where I was chairing a meeting. 'You are killing patients. You are stopping the leukaemics from getting their transfusions.' 'Oh no, I'm not,' I replied, 'You are. Get your staff to do the jobs they are paid to and we will look after the nursing. Now goodbye!' This was one of many skirmishes I had with senior academics and consultants. These were powerful individuals and I did so with much trepidation but it was necessary if we were to establish management control of the hospital.

When I was a junior doctor, the consultant and the ward sister made a formidable partnership. Their powerbases had been eliminated by the NHS management reorganisation in 1974. The BMA and the nurses' trade union, the Royal College of Nursing (RCN), had long demanded that ward sisters be given back their authority. Almost the first thing I told the Chief Nurse was that senior ward nurses would regain control of their areas of responsibility. They would be accountable for ward or clinic hygiene and cleanliness. They would sign off the window cleaning and ensure that the work of the domestics was to their satisfaction and if not, would be expected to require the domestic manager to put matters right. The Director of Nursing said she would be pleased to take this to the senior nurses' meeting. To my surprise their response was lukewarm. Some demanded they should be paid more for supervising non-nursing duties. I spoke at the next Sisters' meeting and reminded them I was seeking to do exactly what their Union had long wanted. The nurses agreed with reluctance; the older Sisters were supportive but the younger ones had no experience of those good old days. When I found a dirty ward or clinic on my walkabouts, I would call both the domestic manager and the ward Sister and remind them of their responsibilities. When I found that windows were not clean, I reminded the Sister that she had signed the chit agreeing they had been cleaned. It was surprisingly hard work to persuade some nurses to become involved in their environment. Some wards and clinics were always spotless and others were not. Ultimately, it was the quality of the ward sister or charge nurse that made the difference. Following the advice and preliminary research by Dr. Iraj Zamiri, one of our microbiologists, we started a hand washing campaign long before the Government took an interest. Several generations of doctors and nurses had become complacent and reliant upon antibiotics, forgetting the importance of simple hygiene and the prevention of cross-infection. I had to listen to a senior surgeon say he wasn't going to have a Persian 'bug' doctor tell him what to do. Now years later the Government is still attempting to correct this problem but, meanwhile, the microbes have become more deadly.

For some years there was an embargo on cleaning windows so they became opaque. The deputy general manager told me that the engineers had reported that the gantry which carried the cage for window cleaners was unsafe and £60K was required to repair it. This was a shock but I told him to proceed. The cleaning contract went out to tender and would also cost a large sum but when the window cleaning started I was soon made aware that the staff knew things were changing. The grass was cut regularly. Where custom and practice had established a path across the grass, a pavement was laid. I prohibited parking on pavements, had bollards inserted and yellow lines laid. Additional car parking space was provided. Wheel clamps were used on illegal parkers and we charged £5 to take them off. A retired policeman was appointed as security officer and given additional staff to monitor the car parks and CCTV screens. Several arrests of car thieves resulted but alas when my car was broken into and the radio taken, that specific camera was not working! Gradually, the appearance of the whole site improved along with the cleanliness of the hospital and the public toilets. Only later did I learn that one of the Concourse toilets had become a meeting place for homosexuals – was their cleanliness the attraction?!

Smoking endangered the staff and patients' health and ward hygiene. As each ward was refurbished, smoking was allowed in one room only or prohibited. It was necessary to refurbish the Coronary Care & Intensive Care Units. David Crosby, a much admired general surgeon, suggested that we should convert the whole of the third floor to look after the high technology clinical services. This was a good idea but it required moving the Professor of Surgery, Les Hughes, an Australian, from a room he used on the third floor and which he opposed vigorously. This produced a swearing competition between us, which ended in a draw. However, we did move him and a costly conversion of the third floor with intensive care, high and low dependency units and coronary care, was completed. I had visited the nurses' restroom in coronary care before the scheme started and had been appalled by the nicotine tar on the walls and air extractors. Before refurbishment was complete, I banned smoking on the whole floor. I was in my office when nurses presented a petition which stated that the ban on smoking in the nurses' restroom was an attack upon their freedom as individuals. I replied that they were nursing patients on coronary and intensive care, many of whom were there because of smoking and I did not consider it reasonable that they should nurse them stinking of cigarette smoke. Those nurses who had to smoke could go downstairs to the Concourse in their break where smoking was permitted. They were sorely aggrieved and accepted my decision with considerable reluctance. Our anti-smoking campaign preceded that of the government.

When I was a junior doctor, and had stopped smoking, cigarette smoke was everywhere in hospitals. It is wonderful now to be free of tobacco smoke in public buildings, but then it was not easy to change long standing habits without the necessary authority. One surgeon continued to smoke cigars in the theatre changing room. Another consultant smoked cigarettes between out-patients. I did not have the authority to stop such habits – all consultant contracts were held by the District Medical Officer. Now I know that I should have put them on a disciplinary charge.

Once our management structure and budget had been given to us by the District Health Authority, we finalised our management team. The only senior members to stay were the nurse and the accountant. Laurence Irving, a first class honours maths graduate, married with one child, became my deputy. The medical staff liked him for he was prepared to negotiate at length until everybody was exhausted and they agreed with him. I frequently told him to get a move on. Mike Lewis at last became our full-time finance officer. Because his qualifications were not Chartered Accountant, the District Finance Officer repeatedly criticised him. However, Mike had forgotten more about UHW finance than the District Finance Officer ever knew. Years later, when the Unit became a Trust, this officer moved from District to be the Trust's Finance Director. He soon took early retirement.

Mike and his team used their computer to identify the expenditure of individual clinical disciplines and, in due course, that of individual procedures, services and investigations. One early consequence was that we identified that surrounding health authorities relied upon the UHW for specialist services such as cardiology. These services were not specifically funded, the costs coming out of our general budget. One example were the pacemakers costing £12K each. I started to request the referring health authority to pay for these before agreeing that the procedure went ahead. After early resistance they agreed. All invoices then were raised by the District Finance Department. We later failed to find evidence that District were crediting the UHW budget for this work and only with considerable difficulty did we discover that District had not sent out the invoices. This was one of many instances of District's acting against the Unit's interest making financial control of our budget most difficult.

The Thatcher Government demanded that health authorities should maximise income generation from NHS facilities. Mike, on his own initiative, with my agreement, had negotiated an agreement with British Airports Authority to develop the Concourse, which required refurbishment, as a shopping area and I was delighted that these negotiations would make a possible £200K profit for each side. I had to get the agreement of Gordon Harrhy to proceed with the deal. After explaining it all, at his request, I left the papers for his signature. I waited and waited for their return – 'Next week' he continually repeated. Finally, after a year's delay we had a row and he came out with the startling, 'Why should UHW get £200K when the other hospitals couldn't?' Within a month the fire regulations were changed and it all became impossible anyway. Much effort had been wasted and an opportunity to earn money for patient care lost. Later, when the UHW became a Trust, a shopping centre was built. Another example was the misuse of NHS staff by the Professor of Haematology. A senior technician had told me that technical haematology NHS staff were doing full-time research instead of clinical work, costing my budget about £150K per annum. To prove this and protect the source of my information, I needed factual evidence about what these laboratory staff were doing. It was necessary to hire an outside organisation, for which I had to get Harrhy's approval. I asked him to sign the contract but he refused, saying he would find me somebody cheaper. Again nothing happened for weeks and finally when I pressed him, he said the Health Authority could not upset its relationship with the College of Medicine. In my opinion several of the senior academics did not fulfil their clinical contracts despite accepting the higher distinction awards in full. The relationship with the College of Medicine and the South Glamorgan Health Authority had made control of the budget extremely difficult.

We had appointed a new Personnel Officer who had a friendly approach, both to me and the staff, and now we had a competent team of six senior managers. Only one, the senior nurse, did not have an office on the management corridor. I was able, therefore, to communicate with everybody and usually immediately. Initially, middle managers had come to me asking me to make decisions for them. After listening I would usually ask them how much they were paid then tell them to go and do their job and make their own decisions. My predecessors apparently had decided everything; (one had left a cupboard full of letters that had not been answered, mostly not even opened.) I reminded them they were now managers and not administrators. I insisted that all managers recognise that we were one team. Whilst they had their own areas of responsibility, if they saw something was wrong, requiring immediate action, they should deal with it or report it to their colleague if they could not do so. The Unit, the hospital and the patient were everybody's priority. Wherever they went, their eyes and ears had to be open. Nobody would be office-bound or blind. They were to be seen and heard. Nowhere was off limits. They, in turn, must get their own staff to adopt the same principles.

I attended the first NHS Management course at Ashbridge, the Management College in Buckingham. This was a significant improvement on Harrogate and gave me an understanding of the massive task ahead and the basics of management and leadership. I recognised I would never become a management guru at this late stage but would have to rely heavily upon common sense and logic in my mission to improve matters. I was determined I would not fail for lack of effort.

I realised that I must not be seen as favouring the doctors in matters of discipline. The Health Authority's disciplinary policy applied to all staff.

Butchers had been sacked for stealing choice cuts, even whole lambs; cleaners or domestic staff who were caught stealing were usually sacked. A small minority of medical staff misbehaved. Verbal abuse by consultants on subordinates was fairly common, particularly the poor telephonists who did their best with a time-expired telephone exchange. I told the head telephonist that if any staff abused them I was to have the name of the alleged offender, who was usually a consultant.

I requested that person to come to see me and as they waited in my secretary's office, she would give them a copy of the disciplinary code open at 'verbal abuse'. They usually looked less than confident when they came in. I discussed the principles of team working, the allegation and how we could either make it a disciplinary matter or they could apologise to the individual concerned. They always chose the latter and I would produce that person from the waiting room and an apology would be made.

The Nurse Director told me that one consultant surgeon was an offender with his ward sister. He repeatedly admitted more patients than there were available beds. When he next lost his temper with the ward sister, he had a call to come to my office, which he did three times in total. He was a likeable, intelligent, hard working individual and usually left my office arm-in-arm with the nurse. He was a colleague I had a lot of time for. He came to see me about starting up laparoscopic surgery for which he had trained in the USA. He made an impressive case that removing a gall bladder this way was followed by two to three days in hospital with ten days off work, as opposed to two or three weeks in hospital and several more off work. I authorised the considerable investment in equipment and never regretted doing so.

Not all of his colleagues were so cooperative. We had purchased a 'Theatre Man' Computer to monitor theatre usage. I learned that a surgeon had refused to operate upon two patients who had already had a pre-med, after a row with his theatre sister. I knew he was regularly absent from one of his weekly clinics and the printout showed that he attended only 50% of his operating lists. He was an irascible character and easily lost his temper. He was shocked by the information I had for him and by my suggestion of referring the matter to the General Medical Council (GMC). He reluctantly agreed to alter his behaviour. Alas he had a coronary thrombosis shortly afterwards and gave up his private practice to become a strong advocate for the NHS. Was this a success for me or a near catastrophe?

Another senior surgeon, of the old school, was in the habit of swearing and throwing his instruments about theatre. At my request he came to see me to talk about this. I reminded him he did not own the instruments or pay to repair their damage. I then hit him hard below the belt. I told him that I had learned that he used the hospital franking machine to send out private practice letters and that the disciplinary policy for theft was dismissal. He was suitably contrite, and the instrument throwing stopped. A junior doctor, who repeatedly failed to pay for her meals in the cafeteria, may not know how lucky she was. I demanded that the Postgraduate Dean remove her immediately. He arranged a transfer to another hospital that day and I often wondered if she had learned a hard lesson. I believe the hospital staff, as a whole, recognised my fairness in these matters; there was a big drop in the various problems brought to my attention.

My walkabouts had raised the standards of cleanliness and general appearance of the hospital. After much prolonged effort we got a new telephone system which eradicated a major source of frustration and anger at the cost of over £1M. Now eighteen years since I retired, I lunch with these colleagues with whom I had these difficulties and I find to my pleasure they do not appear to hold hard feelings about me and these old difficulties. The 'instrument thrower' even said I was the best manager the hospital had!

Every Tuesday afternoon there was a scheduled meeting of the District Health Authority senior managers and the UGMs. This was preceded by a generous buffet lunch, together with wine (providing the DGM and his brother, the Director of Planning were not away playing golf). Each person in turn would brief the meeting about problems or successes. I could guarantee that the UGM of CRI, would criticise the UHW. He never forgave me for being appointed instead of him. The Chairman of the Health Authority, Alan Jones, gave Gordon Harrhy a long rein. Alan was not the sort to delve into the minutiae of the Health Service. The other members of the Authority did little else but attend the Board meetings and chair appointment committees. The two councillors were not seemingly interested in the great strategy but only their own electoral benefit. It was quite usual to see one of them open his Board papers for the first time as he sat down.

My previous experience as consultant on the Area Team and appointment as a General Manager had brought me into conflict with the BMA leadership. I was by now the Chairman of the BMA Welsh Consultants' Committee and still active on the Central Committee and BMA Council. The election of the chair of the Central Committee of the Hospital Medical Services was due and I was asked to stand. In the election there were transferable votes and Brian Lewis, the powerful Vice Chairman, was the first to be eliminated. At the final vote, I came second to Paddy Ross by five votes. Had I been elected I would have resigned my management post and taken up the BMA cudgels for the consultants. That would certainly have been a career change; I might have brought a different approach to BMA thinking.

I had an excellent management team, with one exception. Annette Watkins, our Chief Nurse had suddenly announced her departure – she had been head hunted by the Welsh Office. The Chief Nurse at the DHA advertised twice but we failed to make an appointment. At the third attempt, Gordon Harrhy told us he had been advised by his opposite number at Guy's Hospital that one of the applicants was excellent. The interview panel consisted of an independent nurse, the Health Authority's Chief Nurse, the Chairman, District General Manager and myself. The recommended candidate answered each question to everybody's satisfaction but mine. When I had met him earlier I sensed he said everything he thought I wanted him to say; he seemed just too good. I was the only one of the panel to feel this and Gordon Harrhy repeated the recommendation he had received from Guy's. I said I could not put my finger on it, but I felt there was something wrong with this man. Sadly my anxieties proved to be well founded. The Director of Nursing was office-bound and had other problems. It was not long before I was knocking on Harrhy's door to tell him the facts about this highly recommended nurse. Harrhy accepted the inevitable and transferred him to the Infirmary to a lesser post. There were dirty tricks amongst managers as well.

One morning in the spring of 1989, I picked up the morning post at home. There was an envelope addressed to me from the Prime Minister's office. I thought I was being invited to meet her. To my surprise I read that the Prime Minister was mindful to recommend that the Queen award me an OBE. Would I accept one? I was shocked and delighted. I had to treat the matter confidential. There were stories of awards that had not been announced because somebody talked, so I decided to keep the news to myself. I thought my wife might let her mother know, who in turn would let her sons know, who in turn and so on. It was the hardest task I have had; there were several occasions when I nearly blurted it out. We were flying back from Spain on the day the Birthday Honours were announced. 'Good God,' said Jill reading the paper 'so and so has a gong. They give them to everybody.' 'You had better be careful' I replied, and gave her my letter. She never trusted me again. How dare I keep such news from her! People were very kind; I had a bundle of congratulations to reply to. I learned that the BMA in Wales had put my name forward to the Welsh Office, but the BMA in London regarded it was a reward for being a 'stooge' for Margaret Thatcher. We went to Buckingham Palace that autumn taking Claire and Robert. I found the Investiture very emotional for I seemed to be surrounded by people with severe disabilities who had achieved much. The citation read 'For services to his clinical dis-

Collecting OBE at Buckingham Palace with Robert, Jill and Claire

cipline in Wales and to the involvement of doctors in management'!

In 1989, at an Area Team meeting on a cool summer day, I noticed I was feeling cold and uncomfortable. I was shivering and was pleased when the meeting closed. As I drove home, I became dissociated and lost touch with reality. I ended up at the house of an acquaintance miles away from my home, unaware of who I was or why I was there. She told me to follow her to my home. I had difficulty remembering how to change gear and I found I could not get the car up the drive from the main road. I had profound amnesia and wondered if I was going to die. It did not worry me that I might. Jill questioned me, 'Do you remember going to Buckingham Palace for a medal?' 'Was it a DSO.' I asked. I had been in Spinks for a short while before and had seen a DSO for sale. I could not remember I had an OBE. John Graham, a neurologist, came to see me and arranged for investigations on the next day. They showed that I had raised cholesterol and that a plaque in my left common carotid artery had disintegrated and a piece of it had lodged in my brain. My memory improved daily and I returned to work a week later. It took me some weeks to feel normal, but my memory for names was worsened. Like an idiot I had not done anything about my cholesterol which had been raised for some time. My cholesterol level had been checked at BMA Conferences. I had been advised to see my doctor but had not done so. Shortly after my recovery, a sudden partial loss of vision in my left eye alerted me to the continued danger to my life. It wasn't that I was stupid; it was just that I was too busy to see doctors. In 2009 I found I had continued to be extremely lucky when the complete blockage of my left common carotid artery was found after the vision of my left eye deteriorated.

In 1991, yet another Government reorganisation of the NHS was to be the introduction of autonomous Trusts. To get rid of the dead hand of District Health Authorities was highly attractive to me. Trusts were to have their own Chairman and Board of Directors with the General Manager converted to a Chief Executive. Both the Chairman and District General Manager of the South Glamorgan District Health Authority strongly opposed the proposed autonomous Trusts during the period of consultation. 'Over my dead body' was the Chairman's often repeated phrase. However, the Government decided to proceed despite their objections, though sadly the Chairman, a most pleasant individual, died prematurely. Harrhy asked me to see him. He proposed I would become the Chief Executive for the University Hospital Trust but only if I became full-time. I had been concerned about the Government's proposals for it was obvious that a vast amount of work would fall upon the Chief Executive in setting up a large Trust. I had realised for some time that my several political, clinical and management commitments had combined to tire me out. I was apprehensive of the burden and I had had my little stroke. I was now 61. I did not wish to give up my three clinical sessions for I believed I still had a slim chance of improving on my 'A' distinction award; the salaries for Chief Executives were not yet agreed and I doubted that a full-time post would match clinical salaries – in this I was wrong. I also did not realise I would be able to increase my management support. After thinking the matter over, I told Harrhy that I would not be applying for the post. I ceased to be the UGM of Unit 2 after six years of unremitting slog, leaving the three hospitals in good working order, economically sound and in a far better condition than when I took over. The staff gave me a silver salver as a reminder of these rewarding days, in many ways the most satisfying of my career.

People constantly asked me why I gave up surgery. My reply was that if I made the hospital function properly, more people would benefit than from my one to one clinical relationship with a patient. I believe this to be true. Gordon Harrhy made a generous offer to me. He appointed me to be Director of Medical/Clinical Audit and allotted me extra sessions so that I became full-time on paper. Because I had bought added years and a lump sum, this meant that when I eventually retired at the age of 63, my pension was based on the final salary of full-time with 40 years full paid up service. However, before then I did my time in clinical audit, which was one of several Government initiatives to improve the quality of clinical care.

Several well publicised medical tragedies had highlighted poor outcomes achieved by a minority of consultants who were not subjected to external monitoring, either by their colleagues or an independent body. Medical Audit was the standard practice in the USA but was resisted by many consultants in the UK. Gordon Harrhy made me responsible for its introduction in South Glamorgan but failed to give me the authority to make it work. Medical staff would have one paid session per week committed to audit meetings and work up. Several consultants refused to participate or attend or even allow their juniors to attend. A senior physician at UHW told me that audit was a waste of time because as the UHW was a Teaching Hospital, our practices were the best and what's more, he actually believed what he said. Some consultants refused to change their practices or bad habits despite their failings being identified by audit mostly carried out by their junior staff. These two years were the most unrewarding of my career. I could not increase my clinical sessions for none were available. I found myself wasting time and becoming increasingly bored. I retired on my 63rd birthday, 27 years after being appointed consultant. In retrospect, I made a mistake by refusing the Trust post, for after two months rest my batteries were recharged and my successor was not considered a great success by the clinicians. However, it was too late then. The good news was I did get an 'A+' distinction award, awarded only to 1.2% of consultants, which was compensation.

21 The Management Summary

I have no doubt the tiredness that caused me to reject the Chief Executive post of the proposed UHW Trust was the result of having too many irons in the fire; NHS and private practice, medico legal reports, medical politics and my active participation in the Council and Presidency of the BAOMS, coupled with my difficulties with District management, was too much. However, there were several contributors to my long standing distrust of NHS management.

When I first joined the NHS, Hospital Administrators were exactly that; they carried out the instructions of the Chairman of the Medical Staff Committee and the Board of Governors. Consultants were generally autonomous. The Board Chairman and the governors decided the priorities and the Administrator carried them out until the money ran out, which it did regularly. Consultants ran their own services, developed and delivered them as they wished at their own pace. The acute disciplines had the greatest clout for they were the life and death services, attracting publicity and political support, whereas mental health and community services or dermatology, care of the elderly, and mentally infirm were neglected. Hospitals with Boards of Governors did better than the institutions with Hospital Management Committees. Outside a few physician superintendents, there were few administrators who knew the first thing about medical care. They rarely entered the clinical areas and educationally they were usually at a disadvantage with the doctors. This lack of coherent management produced repeated crises in the hospital service when money ran short in the winter until the new financial year in the spring or the Government responded with one-off payments. Waiting lists were years long. Several NHS reorganisations attempted to put matters right and to increase the power of management. Both main political parties introduced more control from the centre, particularly Labour which always espoused central control of detail. Administrators increased in numbers but not in competence.

In 1974 the American management consultants, Kinsey, were recruited by the Conservative Government to review NHS management, and the principle of line management was introduced. No profession had control over another so that administrators, medicine, nursing, pharmacy and the professions supplementary to medicine, facilities management and so on, were independent of each other. There was no one individual with overall responsibility. Consensus was to rule. The old hierarchy of the consultant, matron and ward sister became impotent. Matron was no longer in overall charge of nursing and cleaning and ward sisters could not give orders to the domestics. At the same time, the trade unions had become more powerful with the Callaghan government and shop stewards found themselves with powers over clinical services and facilities which reached it's height in the 'winter of discontent' in 1973 when only emergency and acute admissions were possible. The medical profession had long regarded administration to be their servant not their master. The few medical managers were the local authority medical Officers of Health from which a few were promoted to hold senior positions in the Government. Clinical staff held public health doctors in low regard and did not consider them 'proper' doctors.

When I came to Wales, the hospital services were organised by the Welsh Hospital Board. I believed that many consultants were in a masonic lodge and I also wondered if being a mason was an important factor in making appointments within the headquarters of what later became the South Glamorgan health Authority. An investigation by the South Wales Echo later disclosed several were in the Penarth Lodge. In due course this Hospital Board was substituted by a Health Directorate in the Welsh Office, staffed by civil servants, with chief officers in medicine, nursing and pharmacy. The Medical Officers of Health, now called community medical staff, were given equal status to consultants and had access to distinction awards. Very few of them were respected by consultants but they had access to Ministers and were politically powerful.

When I was appointed as a consultant in1968, the CRI had one administrator and two assistants plus supporting staff. When the UHW opened in 1971 they moved there but the Government then decided to introduce Health Authorities with delegated powers from the Welsh Office to run all health services in their area. Norman Popplewell resigned and went to Australia and Adrian Evans became the District Administrator of the South Glamorgan Health Authority. As Popplewell's assistants had moved elsewhere, Evans recruited new staff from outside of the NHS, principally a group from organisational and development staff of British Railways. Among them was G.L. Harrhy who had refereed an F.A. Cup Final. The Health Authority staff multiplied and with increased power. The senior posts duplicated those in the Welsh Office Health Directorate, whilst middle or junior rank administrators were put in day-to-day charge of the hospitals according to their size.

Throughout this long period, the Government failed to set up a collegiate body to pick and train qualified personnel in hospital management. Although there was now a career pathway, there was no training comparable to that provided in the armed forces or by the medical Royal Colleges. Administrative experience was gained in post with the result that very few capable staff surfaced and those who did, did not know what the doctors did, how they worked or what was required by the population at large.

This may explain why, when I was appointed as a consultant, I did not have a job plan or a timetable and was left to develop my own service. In 1980 I was elected Chairman of the Medical Board and took my seat on the Area Team of the health authority. Adrian Evans was a chapel-going teetotaller, an earnest individual, driven to the point of nervous collapse by his Team colleagues who rotated the chair every three months as they tried to achieve consensus. The Director of Finance was deaf and had come from Local Government. The Medical Officer had the habit of disappearing for long periods when he was needed. The Estates Manager wrote long reports that rarely reached a recommendation. The Team itself debated at length and achieving consensus was time consuming.

The one good thing, I remember, was the Team lunch that preceded the weekly Team meeting. Their quality was excellent and the drinks non-alcoholic. Two female caterers produced the meals over which the patriarch Raymond Cory presided as chairman. One of the puddings was usually a Black Forest gateau which always appealed to Adrian Evans. One day one of the caterers asked to speak to me in confidence. Did I know Mr. Evans was strongly opposed to alcohol? Did I know they made extra gateaux for Mr. Evans to consume at home. I said 'Yes' to the first and 'No' to the second. She was very worried because she put a lot of sherry in the gateau. Should she tell him? 'Of course not,' I said. I found the idea of a militant abstainer delighting in the alcohol of a Black Forest gateaux highly amusing. Perhaps Adrian should have had more alcohol to calm his nerves for the difficulties of the job proved to be too much and he took early retirement on health grounds. His two assistants, Gordon Harrhy and Alan Trew, vied for the vacant post both without experience of working in hospital, general practice or public health clinics.

Raymond Cory soon retired and Alan Jones, a solicitor and former Tory parliamentary candidate replaced him. Like Raymond, Alan was a likeable person who allowed Gordon freedom of action. Alcohol was now served with our lunches and, again, often after meetings from a well stocked sideboard. Alcohol before a meeting was not a good idea. After the 1984 Griffiths Management Enquiry and the introduction of general management, Gordon became District General Manager. His brother John, became the Director of Planning.

When I took over the UHW, the acting deputy manager was a delightful person whose efficiency was significantly affected by his regular habit of popping down to the local at lunchtime for a pint or two. When I first smelt alcohol on his breath I told him I would not tolerate this habit but he could not stop it. I did not appoint him to the substantive post and he returned to District Headquarters.

Alan Trew, the Unit General Manager at the Cardiff Royal Infirmary repeatedly attacked the UHW or me directly at Team meetings. The failure of the government and the NHS to establish a proper career structure and training system for management following the inception of the NHS in 1948 must be the principal reason for the failure of management over the first 50 NHS years. There were several attempts to bring in senior managers from industry or retired officers of the armed forces, but few were successful in dealing with a workforce that was usually better educated and knew more about the work than they did. Service officers, long used to giving orders, were frustrated by clinicians who refused to obey them. Until the Trusts were formed, consultants' contracts were held in the Regional or District Headquarters which was an added difficulty in managing consultants and their activities.

How was it that I was reasonably successful when I had no in-depth management training or experience? I had certainly tucked away in my memory bank my father's style in communication and meeting his staff and his demand that they did their job properly to the highest standard. My parents repeatedly told me, 'If a job is worth doing, it is worth doing properly.' This drove me wild as a child but this is what I practised in my clinical work and I used to say, 'If it looks good, it probably is.' I applied this to my management style.

Most consultants aspire to be leaders in their field and of their junior staff. They expect their wishes to be carried out. They are used to taking a decision without too much delay and to stick by that decision. The consequences may be painful for the patient, but the decision is meant to be in the patient's long term interest. A lot of prior information may be necessary in order to take that decision and sometimes the decision is to wait and see. It remains a decision. Taking a decision was relatively easy for me as a manager. Many lay administrators/managers rarely ventured into clinical areas. They rarely talked to their staff; whole areas of clinical practice were unknown to them. Many were in awe of senior clinicians and more so if they were professors. I was able to take on professors and consultants who abused the service even though I was initially very apprehensive when I did.

As a clinician nowhere was off limits to me. The Professor of Paediatrics asked me what I was doing on his ward. I reminded him it was an NHS ward, not his. Because I went everywhere and immediately drew the attention of those responsible to problems, the hospital became clean and pleasing to work in; staff could see there was a difference. It took some time and much effort to achieve this but it was simple leadership, not atomic physics. Being a clinician was crucial to my success and I wish more senior doctors were in senior management. Unfortunately, in my day no thought had been given to the career prospects of senior clinicians who moved into management. If you were a clinical full-time manager, you were not considered further for a Distinction Award. If you retained three or more sessions you were. Until the Trusts were introduced there was little chance of achieving a comparable salary to clinicians. Management became less satisfying as central government issued more and more instructions, targets and quotas, and most clinicians became deeply frustrated by the management decisions. Managing doctors and nurses and satisfying the needs of government was extremely difficult so that, as the government made more and more management decisions, the majority of clinical managers returned to their clinical specialties. However, the introduction of clinical directors of service disciplines and medical directors at board level was a major contribution to healthcare management. Alas the centralised management espoused by Labour governments eroded their function, leading to the breakdown of some clinical services in the first decade of this century.

Some clinical managers forgot they were clinicians and that ethical quality care of patients was their number one priority. Because of this an increasing number of NHS disasters filled the headlines.

22 Chairman of Glan-y-Môr NHS Trust and the Battle for Neath General Hospital

After a wonderful retirement dinner, given by my colleagues, for six weeks my wife had the luxury of having me about the house. We were not used to being together so much and it proved not to be a bed of roses. One morning I had a phone call from Peter Gregory, the NHS Director of the Welsh Office, asking if I was interested in being the Chairman of the NHS Trust covering the Neath and Port Talbot area. I admitted that my knowledge of the area consisted of driving through it and along the new bypass. However, I was interested. He invited me to an interview the next day. At the Welsh Office I was shown into a room to meet Peter Gregory, the Director, Colin Williams his number two, the Chief Medical Officer Deidre Hine and Chief Nursing Officer Marion Bull.

Peter said that there had been difficulty in finding a Chairman for the Trust, which brought together the acute, community and mental health services for the area. Did I know anything about them? I replied, 'As Chairman of the Welsh CCHMS I had listened repeatedly to the Swansea consultants attacking the principle of the projected four Trusts for the area.' They had wanted one Trust and they sought to centralise hospital services for West Glamorgan in Swansea. I wished I had listened more carefully to their arguments.

Peter then asked me if I would be able to cope with the introduction of a new model of clinical services for the projected new General Hospital, that was opposed by the existing consultant body, and get the long delayed replacement for the time-expired Neath General Hospital built against the opposition of the consultant body in Swansea and the local government of Neath and Port Talbot.

He explained that the opposition for a projected 350 bed local general hospital and the model of clinical service which had been agreed by the Secretary of State for Wales came from not only the Swansea and Neath consultants, but also the local Labour Councils who wanted a 550 bed District General Hospital with all major clinical services. This united, but disparate, opposition had caused long delays in setting up the Trust and the new hospital planning.

I replied that as the Unit General Manager at the University Hospital of Wales, I had won the support of consultants in order to improve services, despite making controversial change and that at the BMA I had taken an unpopular lead in pressing for the clinical involvement in NHS management. I was used to being on the wrong side of the table as far as clinical colleagues were concerned and, as for the local Council, I would persuade them by argument backed by the special knowledge I had as a hospital doctor and manager. Little did I understand local Labour politics. After a two-way discussion, I was told that Peter Gregory would discuss the matter with the Minister.

About a week later I received a call to go up to the Welsh Office in Whitehall, London. There I met Rod Richards, the Minister for Health, who was very friendly and spoke as if I was already the Chairman. He gave me two priorities, to get the Trust to work and to find out what was holding up the new hospital and get it built.

With that he gave me a handshake and a goodbye smile. It was a tragedy for him and for Wales that his political career foundered because of personal problems. He was a doer.

After my appointment as Chair was announced in the Western Mail, I set off to meet the Chief Executive, Andrew Bellamy, in Swansea where the headquarters were situated. Andrew had previously been the General Manager of Neath General Hospital and we had met many times. I was to know him well, like him and appreciate his many qualities. He was a good administrator but he had found the pressure of the setting up of a new Trust, in the face of the combined opposition of clinicians and politicians without the support of a Chairman, a heavy burden. He had found himself isolated when the Chairmen and CEOs of the four Trusts met. For my part, I had to remember that a Non Executive Chairman had to keep himself out of the detail of the day-to-day running of the Trust. Within a short time we made a successful duo, for I took much of the political and media pressure off him and his team, allowing them to form and run the new Trust, which made a formidable task in itself. One of our early tasks was to name the Trust Glan-y-Môr. The seaside.

Glan-y-Môr was a fusion of two service units previously managed independently: Neath General Hospital, a DGH being one Unit and the combined mental health and community services for West Glamorgan the other. Glan-y-Môr brought them under one management and we had to make them gel. In addition, the business case for the replacement hospital had to be written in a manner which satisfied in turn the West Glamorgan Health Authority, the Welsh Office and the Treasury. Soon the Private Finance Initiative replaced central funding and took us further into unchartered waters. Not only, therefore, did the Trust management have to amalgamate two separate Units cohesively and within budget, but also had to prepare a preliminary business case for a new hospital using an unknown system. That the Trust succeeded in doing both was a triumph for which its senior management received little recognition, which was disgraceful.

The Trust's offices were sited in Swansea, well away from any of our hospitals and most clinics. Andrew had to complete his senior team and I had to get to know the patch. The Trust covered a wide geographical area, all of which was unknown to me. I knew little about community care, care of the elderly, mental or physical disability, or acute mental health. The acute services provided by Neath General Hospital were not a problem but I admit to finding initially that some patients of acute mental health, care of the elderly and mentally infirm disturbing; as Chairman I had to take an active interest in all disciplines and their patients. I started my walkabouts, paying the same attention to patient care, staff morale, cleanliness and window cleaning as I had in Cardiff.

At the earliest opportunity I met the senior clinical staff. At a packed meeting in Neath General of consultants, senior nurses, support staff and therapists, I outlined my priorities and my determination to achieve them. I talked about the new model of clinical services for the new hospital, the need for team work, the importance of Glan-y-Môr Trust and building the new hospital. I complimented the staff on what I had seen since I arrived. The questioning that followed opened with a diatribe from Dr. Dewi Evans, a Swansea based consultant paediatrician and Plaid Cymru politician. He attacked the concept of the Trust, the new hospital and the clinical services. 'Patient care demanded that the Trust and clinical services should be centered in Swansea,' he said. I responded by saying, 'Anyone who did not wish the Trust to succeed should 'bugger off' elsewhere as several had already. We did not want them. People could either be with us or against us.' Several heads nodded in support. When Dr Evans withdrew to Swansea we had to defeat his attempts to take all the Neath paediatric services with him. Our paediatric intensive care had already gone to Swansea for good clinical reasons. I left all present at the meeting in no doubt of my determination that the Trust would succeed and the new hospital be built.

This meeting almost stopped the flow of Neath consultants to Swansea where I later discovered the management of Singleton and Morriston Hospitals, with the support of their consultants, were developing clinical services and facilities in the expectation that Neath General Hospital was to close with its financial resources transferred to them. They now headhunted our breast surgeon, although he did retain outpatient sessions at Neath. Ten Neath consultants had left to work in Swansea and one, Hugh Williams, a Neath General Urologist, had died prematurely and one went elsewhere. It was not unreasonable for them to believe that the new hospital would not be built, despite its 20 year gestation. They decamped for better pasture, or so they thought.

My next meeting of note was with senior members of the Neath and Port Talbot Council, all old Labour and hostile. Their leader was Noel Crowley. He started, not with a greeting, but an aggressive statement including a swear word. He saw me as a lackey of Mrs. Thatcher send down from Cardiff to shut Neath General, stop the new hospital building and send everything to Swansea. He wanted a new, fully staffed 550 bed DGH and he did not care what a Tory Secretary of State wanted or said. He worked on the principle that what Swansea had Neath had to have. I was taken aback by this hostility and lack of comprehension, and in my ignorance I decided to keep cool, keep the peace and give a reasoned reply. I explained the reality of modern patient care, future medical staffing problems and money shortages. I repeated the priorities I had been given. It was wasted on him but some of his colleagues appeared to listen and understand. I was to learn this was his standard approach. Seven years later I lost my temper and let rip at him verbally, which produced a major change in his behaviour. I should have had the row with him at the outset instead of trying to be reasonable. I was new to the job and lacked the knowledge of how to deal with old style local Labour politicians in a one party state. I believed then we had to build bridges to gain their cooperation and bring them into the world of healthcare run by the Welsh Office and later the National Assembly. It took a long time, but I believe we succeeded with the one exception of Crowley.

The Welsh Office's Health Department forecast that the several district general hospitals scattered about Wales could not be properly staffed or afforded and that some acute services were better centralised in order to maintain quality care. Several years earlier, the Royal College of Surgeons had reviewed the emergency surgical services in West Glamorgan following a number of problems. The College had recommended the centralisation of acute emergency and trauma surgery in Morriston hospital, which already housed neurosurgery, plastic and maxillofacial surgery, general surgery and orthopaedics. This recommendation was based on clinical common sense and had resulted in the A&E Department at Neath General Hospital being downgraded to a local accident centre dealing with trauma not requiring hospital admission. The Secretary of State had further decided that acute emergency surgery would close at Neath and that the annual 6,000 emergency medical admissions would continue. Paediatric admissions and intensive care would go to Swansea, leaving a paediatric day unit in Neath. What was left, including uncomplicated obstetrics and gynaecology, was to be the role of the proposed new local general hospital. The Leader of the Neath Port Talbot council opposed these changes and, ignoring our staffing difficulties, demanded that Neath must have all full services. The paediatrician, Dewi Evans, continued to demand that all children's services should leave Neath. At the first meeting of the West Glamorgan Trust Chairmen and CEOs that I attended, it was agreed that the new hospital would never be built. I repeated that my intension was to ensure it was. I did not realise then just how far advanced Singleton and Morriston Trusts were in their plans to take over our services.

The Private Finance Initiative (PFI) was a developing process with the Treasury altering the rules with every new scheme for a school, bridge, road or hospital. Money was to be raised in the private sector with the risks of the scheme transferred from the NHS to the successful bidder. It sounded easy, but its negotiations were complex for both sides and for a small Trust also managing health services, a mammoth task. In essence, it is arranging a mortgage for a multi-million project to be paid back over 30 years, the half life of the hospital.

The Trust first had to finalise what facilities would be required to deliver the services stipulated by the Secretary of State within the overall budget, approved by the Health Authority. We then advertised for interested parties across the European Union to submit preliminary drawings. Negotiations started to make the choice of a preferred bidder. Satisfying the Health Authority, Welsh Office and Treasury were the least of the problems for our negotiating team. We not only had to keep our clinicians fully involved in drawing up the specifications but there were the usual day-to-day problems of clinical care.

In that summer of 1996 the first of many crises occurred. Singleton recruited another of our general surgeons, making the surgical cover for surgical emergencies unsafe. The physicians then came to see us to tell us that they could not accept medical emergencies without adequate surgical cover for the few cases requiring immediate surgery, e.g. an acute bleeding gastric ulcer. As we had already lost several anaesthetists to Swansea, we were in a desperate situation. I suggested that we should bring forward the proposed transfer of emergency surgery immediately and try to recruit consultant surgeons and anaesthetists as soon as possible for the elective work. I believed that consultants nearing the end of their careers would find the absence of night and weekend working attractive. Thankfully, the Health Authority agreed the change of plan and our overburdened finance director set to to determine what emergency surgery cost us to deliver. I insisted we played it straight and a sum of £1.3m was identified and transferred from our budget to Morriston. Their general surgeons agreed to provide the surgical cover required by our physicians but only if patients requiring surgery were transferred to their hospital. Reluctantly, along with our physicians, we agreed, and acute surgical emergencies were no longer referred to Neath General. At the last minute, and without warning, the Morriston surgeons withdrew their agreement to cover our medical admission, with the result that the majority of our physicians again wanted to stop medical admissions. Fortunately, the senior physician wished to keep Neath open and his two colleagues reluctantly agreed to continue until we could appoint our surgeons.

We appointed two experienced consultant anaesthetists, one from Sweden. We shortlisted three applicants for the surgical jobs. One was our existing locum consultant; another was a British surgeon who was returning from Saudi Arabia. Both were middle aged and experienced but had had atypical training as juniors because of job shortages. The third applicant was an NHS consultant in the North of England who wanted to return to Wales. I went on my summer holiday content with the knowledge that my Vice Chairman would Chair the Advisory Appointment Committee and we would appoint three surgical consultants. I returned to learn that the Royal College representative had refused to take into account the surgical careers and experience of the two and had concluded that without a standard certificate of surgical training they could not be appointed; only one consultant applicant had been successful.

I gave instructions to re-advertise immediately and at the earliest opportunity we had a shortlist of two – the two surgeons previously interviewed. I telephoned the new Royal College representative and explained the necessity of making these appointments in order to keep the hospital open. He appeared to agree with me. I chaired the interview and it seemed to go well. Questions from the Committee and the College representative about applicants' careers, their surgical training and experience were answered satisfactorily. I was unprepared when decision time came and both the Swansea and the RCS surgeon said that without training certificates neither candidate was appointable. When neither would change their position, I reminded the meeting that this was a Trust appointment and that this was an Advisory Appointment Committee and that I would take a vote. It was two for and two against. I then used my vote to make it 3:2 in favour. I said the recommendation would go to the next Trust Board meeting which, of course, confirmed the appointments. I was certain the Swansea surgeons had got to the Royal College representative after I had talked to him. We then received a copy of a letter from the College representative to the College President asserting that these appointments were a miscarriage of procedure. I did not have to, but I wrote seeking a meeting with the President in London. There I reminded him that one of the appointees had been in post for several years as a locum consultant, covering, on many occasions his consultant colleagues. I stressed both their FRCS and their surgical backgrounds – one had trained in the USA and been a consultant in the Middle East, and the other was already a respected surgeon in Neath. I slipped in that these were

Board appointments and that I had a priority to keep the hospital open. The President, perhaps recognising the inevitable, wished me, his surgical colleagues and the Trust well. We heard no more from the College.

The hospital was saved and the physicians pacified. Later when I met Colin Williams, the number two of the Welsh Office, he told me that he had expected to find the hospital shut and padlocked when he returned from his summer leave; I felt that I had demonstrated the value of having a retired clinician as Chairman. Had the hospital closed we would never have had its replacement. In my discussions with the medical director I stressed the importance of recording and auditing everything our surgeons did.

Trust Chairmen can do as much or as little as they wish, but if the Trust is to be successful they must do more than chair the Board meetings. There are many mundane tasks, one being the development of relationships with the civic authorities. I sought to have regular meetings with the full Neath Port Talbot Council so that we could explain what was happening in the NHS Wales and their own Trust. I was not successful. Their leader did not wish his colleagues to know what was happening.

In the early months of my chairmanship of Glan-y-Môr Andrew and I had several meetings with a group of politicians who remained opposed to what they regarded as a downgrading of Neath General. Noel Crowley's favourite description was 'a cottage hospital'. He resolutely refused to see any advantage in the proposals. Through the auspices of the Neath Port Talbot Borough Council, a public meeting was arranged. Peter Hain, the MP for Neath, came in that afternoon for a full briefing on what was proposed, why and where and how much progress had been made. We were at pains to correct all of his misunderstandings and answer every question. As we left to go to the meeting, Peter said to me 'Don't worry about the rhetoric.' At the meeting after I explained the proposals, I was assailed verbally by the Socialist Workers and other groups. Finally, Hain stood up and spoke at length. He criticised everything we were attempting to do. He was not speaking about the hospital but his next election. He attacked the existence of PFI and demanded central funding. He could not support a project of the Conservative Government. His speech was a cynical abuse of truth and I realised, yet again, just what being a professional politician meant.

I repeatedly told the meeting that if a new hospital was wanted in Neath/Port Talbot this was the only one they would get. The silent majority gave us their support by the end of the meeting. I was not surprised by Hain's 'volte face' when the New Labour Government adopted the same approach, but calling it a public private partnership or PPP; nor was

I surprised when he had later to resign from the Cabinet.

The bilateral agreement to transfer emergency surgery to Swansea, agreed by the Health Authorities, included the transfer back of 400 elective waiting list cases from Swansea to Neath. This would have eased the financial loss to Glan-y-Môr Trust and reduced the Swansea waiting lists. Swansea did not keep their side of this agreement which aggravated our financial position and precipitated an exchange of correspondence between myself and Keith Vaughan, their medical director, in March 1997.

On October 27th 1997, Colin Ferguson, the Secretary of the Swansea Division of Surgery, wrote to the CEO of the West Glamorgan Health Authority alleging that the quality of surgical services in Neath did not match that of Swansea, and he criticised our cancer and vascular services in particular. We had already heard rumours of criticisms made at dinner parties by Swansea surgeons and had reviewed our audit material thoroughly to determine if these criticisms were justified. As no such evidence existed, I pressed the Health Authority to carry out a district wide audit of the outcome of surgery and this was agreed in November 1997, when a review of general surgical services was commenced by Dr. Peter Donnelly, the Director of Public Health Medicine to the Health Authority.

In December 1997, Colin Ferguson wrote to the Authority stating it would not be productive to compare the results of surgery between hospitals in West Glamorgan but he renewed his criticism of our surgical services. In July 1998, we learned that a delegation of Swansea surgeons, led by Professor John Baxter, had specifically criticised the competence and standards of surgery in Neath at a meeting with the Chief Medical Officer, Dr. Ruth Hall, at the Welsh Assembly. They could not provide information to back up their criticisms. Dr. Hall then demanded an immediate investigation to determine the facts and I too demanded to know what was the basis for these allegations, for I had a duty of care for our patients, required by the GMC, as I was still a medical practitioner.

On 15th July 1998, the CEO of the Health Authority confirmed, when writing to me, that the Medical Director of Morriston had criticised the surgical services at Neath but added that he had no first-hand knowledge and had relied upon remarks made by other colleagues! By September these allegations began to unravel. Professor Baxter, in a memorandum dated 16th September, admitted that neither Singleton nor Morriston Hospitals had a robust mechanism for collecting their surgical data. On 25th September, the Medical Director of Morriston wrote that no criticism of Neath consultants was or had been intended. On 3rd November, the CEO of the Health Authority regretted the length of time required to acquire the audit data from the Swansea and Morriston Trusts, which of course should have been immediately available as the result of four years of medical audit, supposed to have been done in both hospitals.

Finally, their criticisms of our surgical cover were withdrawn after the investigation by the Director of Public Health Medicine found that the allegations of incompetence made to Dr. Ruth Hall could not be substantiated and that the surgical audit information available at Neath was significantly better than elsewhere in West Glamorgan. In January 1999, I wrote to my fellow Chairman in West Glamorgan, to advise them that if I heard of further criticism of our surgeons from their staff, I would refer the matter to the GMC. In 'Fitness to Practise', the GMC stated 'criticism of fellow doctors must be capable of being substantiated.' To all intents and purposes this closed this matter and was proof that information is power. Monitoring and auditing our surgical activity had been justified by events. Our critics did not stop their unprofessional behaviour entirely. In 2001, the new President of the RCS visited the nearly completed replacement for Neath General after visiting Swansea. He took me aside and told me that he had heard that our emergency vascular surgery was not up to standard. I asked for details of these allegations and followed this by a letter to him repeating my request. I did not get a reply. Was it not strange that Swansea later attempted to include our vascular surgeon in their emergency rota?

These unsavoury episodes are an example of the depths some doctors will sink to in order to achieve their aim, which in this case was the closure of surgical services in Neath and the cancellation of the new hospital. When it was opened, the Swansea consultants changed their tack. They proposed that the hospital should be transferred to the Swansea Trust. When that failed, they said all surgical services should be merged so that Swansea's waiting list patients could have their surgery in the new hospital. It should be remembered that they had reneged on their agreement to transfer 400 such cases in 1996. Finally, they wanted our surgeons, whom they had previously criticised, to be part of their emergency rotas. The Bro Morgannwg Trust ,which was now managing the Neath Port Talbot Hospital, rejected all of these proposals and was able to protect the integrity of the hospital and its services.

I remain convinced that there was a tacit agreement between the Swansea and Morriston Hospital managements and their consultants that they would bring about the closure of Neath General Hospital. The management let the clinicians fire the bullets whilst they cleaned their weapons. Had Neath General closed with the cancellation of the replacement hospital, it is certain that the two Swansea hospitals would not have been able to cope with the 6,000 medical emergencies that were admitted annually to Neath. As it was, the pressure arising from dealing with our surgical emergencies caused major difficulties and lengthened the waiting lists at Swansea. It was also the basis of a new financial scandal. Our Trust had £1.3m deducted from our budget by the Authority, being the true cost of our emergency surgical services. When Swansea demanded £3.5m to do the same work I repeatedly pointed out that Morriston Hospital had expanded its surgical services and facilities in preparation for the closure of Neath General. For example, they had allocated an additional half ward to maxillofacial surgery in Morriston, despite not receiving additional maxillofacial work from Neath. The public outcry at the financial difficulties of Morriston and their failure to reduce waiting lists resulted in a House of Commons visitation composed almost entirely of Swansea district MPs. Nobody from Glan-y-Môr was called and when I complained about this, the Chairman of the Health Authority, Hugh Thomas, said he did not wish to have 'our dirty linen washed in public.' Glan-y-Môr had no dirty linen! There was plenty of it nearby however.

My repeated complaint to the Authority that the Glan-y-Môr Trust and its patients were being short changed, was strengthened by the Commons visit and the resulting extra £4m given to Swansea in addition to capital funding. To compensate for this, other Health Authorities in Wales were given extra money by the Assembly. Every Trust but Glan-y-Môr benefitted. Our patients were punished by a double whammy as we could not provide the services enjoyed by the patients of the continually overspent Swansea Trust. In 2009 the wheel had turned and the Swansea and Bro Morgannwg Trusts merged with the dominant successful management of Bro Morgannwg in charge of the Abertawe Bro Morgannwg Trust. Unfortunately the budget deficit was also merged.

Whilst all this nasty business was on-going, the negotiations and planning for the new hospital continued until finally the outline business case was complete. The next stage was to complete the specifications and choose the preferred bidder, all of which involved considerable effort from the senior Trust management and expense. Fortunately, the money supporting this negotiation, the legal and other services, came from the Welsh Office and later the Assembly. Towards the end of this expensive negotiation, the 1997 General Election returned a Labour Government traditionally opposed to PFI. Perhaps because of the considerable investment already made, the scheme was not cancelled by the new Welsh Minister for Health, Jane Hutt.

The consortium of a Swansea building company, a facilities management firm and group of architects was chosen as preferred bidder. They set up the Baglan Moor Healthcare plc. The planning, design and preparation for the building and final business case could now start. This coincided with a decision of the new Wales Government to consult on the reduction of 30 Trusts to 16. It was proposed that Swansea and Morriston would be one Trust and Glan-y-Môr would combine with Bridgend. I did not support this proposal for I believed the proposed new Trust was unlikely to be supportive of the new hospital as I remembered the earlier stated views of the Trust Chairman. I did not believe I would be appointed to the Chair of the new Trust as I was not a member of the Labour Party (or any other) and the Leader of Neath Port Talbot County Borough Council was certainly not my supporter. When the Secretary of State for Wales and the local MP, Peter Hain, sent a joint letter to the local paper during the period of consultation advocating a union between Glan-y-Môr and Bridgend, I responded critically. They were infuriated and I knew then that I was finished. Jane Hutt confirmed the Trust proposal and Glan-y-Môr and Bridgend Trusts were to be merged, minus the acute metal health services of Swansea.

23 The Impact of the New Labour Government of 1997

The New Labour landslide of the General Election of 1997 also provided a Labour administration in Wales. We had a new Minister of Health, Jane Hutt. She was earnest, dedicated and well meaning.

Early in the Labour administration, the 30 Trusts were reduced to 16 and later the 5 Health Authorities were to be replaced by 30 Local Health Boards. The NHS advised caution because of the paucity of good management staff and setting up costs (estimated at £68m). There were several immediate adverse consequences for the Trusts. Neighbouring Local Health Boards (LHB) had differing priorities and spending plans detrimental to the Trusts' recruitment of clinical staff.

Some LHBs could not control their GP drug budget and withdrew money from Trusts to pay for this. The quality of LHB Chairmen and CEOs was extremely variable. Jane had persuaded potential Chairmen of LHBs that they would have autonomy and the authority to go with it. When I co-chaired the first joint meeting of Chairmen, I could not believe their 'naivety'. Had they not heard of waiting list targets, budget deficits and so on? Did they not realise they would be managed from The Welsh Assembly in Cardiff Bay? I told them that Trust autonomy had disappeared under New Labour. Did they know health investment in Wales was half that of England? Their response was that Jane had given them autonomy. Soon the NHS in Wales went deeper into the mire with increasing waiting lists and financial deficits.

About this time I was invited, with many others, to 10 Downing Street to celebrate the modernisation of the NHS. I found myself standing next to Cherie Blair, who wanted to know where Bro Morgannwg was. After telling her I said that I felt a fraud being there for Wales had not yet modernised its NHS. 'Yes,' she said, 'We are all worried about Wales.'

The Chairman of the West Glamorgan Health Authority, Hugh Thomas, was affectionately known as 'Hugh Bach'. He took me out to lunch; I noticed he had a habit of giving a warm welcome whilst looking over the shoulder to see who else was there. He told me that he was considering applying for the vacant Chair of the Swansea Trust. In our discussions he surprised me by telling me he believed that the CEO of Iechyd Morgannwg Health Authority, Jan Williams, proposed to advise their Board that the so called Baglan Hospital should not be built. If this threat was true it was not carried out. I already believed that the Health Authority had done its best to frustrate our efforts during the negotiations for the new hospital. Months earlier we had learned that our breast service in Neath was to be transferred to Swansea. The Glan-y-Môr Trust had not been consulted but Jan Williams had already had discussions with our breast surgeon. Neath had long had an effective, innovative one-stop breast clinic, highly valued by patients and GPs. I decided to involve the local politicians on this occasion and a minor storm was created. I had a face to face with Jan Williams. Her response was unusual – she exclaimed that she wanted to improve breast services because of these, pointing to her own breasts. They were an impressive argument but did not persuade me that Neath women should lose their proven service. The proposal was withdrawn. Perhaps wishing to protect the Prince Philip Hospital in Llanelli, where she had worked, Jan Williams was prepared to sacrifice the Baglan Hospital. Our working relationship never recovered from this row over breast services. I have to report, however, that later one of her colleagues Eiffion Williams who became our Director of Finance denied that Mrs. Williams had wished to scupper the hospital.

I applied for the Chairmanship of the new Trust but without hope. What I had not realised was that I had considerable support from the Glan-y-Môr Board and also from some local politicians. Senior management in Bridgend must also have been supportive. Satisfying the Nolan principles, I was interviewed by the Minister and her Committee and to my surprise was appointed. I believe my appointment owed much to the success of the Glan-y-Môr Trust and the need to persuade the Neath and Port Talbot staff that this would be a merger with and not a takeover by Bridgend and that the new hospital would remain a priority.

There were few perks in a chairmanship but an annual day out resulted from an invitation of the Royal College of Physicians to a propaganda meeting at their college followed by an excellent dinner. I met chairpersons from the UK and realised from our conversations and their questions how little they knew about health care.

At one dinner I sat beside the Vice President, a gastro-enterologist and lamented that male medical staff were no longer chaperoned. He said his private practice was at his home and he was chaperoned by his wife. Once, as he examined a female bowel through a sigmoidoscope, the front door bell rang and his wife left the room. Alas, she didn't shut the door properly and he realised that their golden retriever was standing quite close wagging its tail. Not knowing what to do he said nothing and carried on with his examination. Out of the corner of his eye he saw the dog licking an exposed buttock. His wife returned at that time and removed the dog. Nothing was said either by the patient or him and he still wondered what went through her mind as she dressed. It was an extreme example but it confirmed the need for chaperones!

24 The Bro Morgannwg Trust, a Difficult Start but a Strong Finish

With my appointment as Chairman Elect, came two non-executive directors from Glan-y-Môr and two from Bridgend. Three new non-executives were to be appointed later. One of my first tasks was to take part in the appointment of the Chief Executive. Peter Gregory chaired the appointments committee. Paul Williams, the Chief Executive of Bridgend, was extremely nervous and did not interview well but his track record was excellent and, with the strong support of Peter Gregory, he got a unanimous vote. This was good politics as we now had a Chairmen Elect from Glan-y-Môr and Chief Executive Elect from Bridgend. Could we make it work?

Paul had some general discussions with me before our respective appointment committees; although I had met him many times before, I had no in-depth knowledge of him as a person. My general impressions were that he was reserved, didn't smile much, perhaps even dour. The day after his appointment we met at the Trust Headquarters in Bridgend in what had been the Nurses' Home for Bridgend General Hospital. During our conversation he said he had had two excellent Chairmen before me who had left him alone to manage whilst they ran the Board meetings. It didn't take a genius to get his message. I replied that I had already had experience of being a Non Executive Chairman of Glan-y-Môr and didn't intend that to change. However, I had also been a Health Service clinician and manager and that he should not expect me to behave in the same manner as my predecessors. We agreed on the principle of my 'needing to know'. I was not to be faced with a political or media crisis about which I knew nothing. We parted on reasonable, if wary terms.

Because of my increasing osteoarthritis, which had already resulted in a hip replacement in 1996, the Chairman and Chief Executive offices were switched from the top to the ground floor of this sound and substantial building, for which I was grateful. In order to dampen the suspicions of the Neath Port Talbot staff about a takeover, we had thought of renting an office block half way between the two main towns, but I could not see the point of leaving such a substantial building. To save money we stayed put. Paul prepared his proposed management structure and agreed it with me. We made his Executive appointments and I toured the areas I did not know, including Maesteg and the neighbouring valleys. I made walkabouts through the larger hospitals. My impression of the Princess of Wales Hospital in Bridgend was that the physical facilities were good, modern and successful but overall the hospital's cleanliness was poor. Glanrhyd Hospital, the mental health institution, set in delightful surroundings, was composed of separate buildings sited around a large central area of grass and mature trees. It was well past its sell-by date even though some excellent ward conversions had been completed. I was badly affected when I visited a large dormitory full of beds and lockers without evidence of their use. When I asked why this ward was not used, I was told it was used every night. When I questioned the absence of evidence of any personal belongings, the reply was that those patients were not the sort to have or look after their belongings. The eyes of the senior nurse telling me this made me suddenly think of a concentration camp, although I am sure she did not mean ill towards her patients.

On my next visit to Headquarters, I reported to Paul on my travels. I said I had become used to clean hospitals in Glan-y-Môr where we had an excellent Domestic Manager and that I was not impressed by what I had seen in the Princess of Wales Hospital and elsewhere. I told him I had been informed that in order to save money, the domestic and healthcare workers had been converted into a single post with both functions. The ward sisters had been unanimous that this did not work. Inevitably with nursing absences, the healthcare assistants (HCAs) spent more time on patient care than cleaning and the ward sister claimed they could do nothing to correct this. This was a tricky situation for me, as this scheme had been the product of the Human Resources Director of the then Bridgend Trust who was the same person in that post at the UHW when I had been appointed as General Manager. Paul said my predecessor had not made similar comments despite spending much time in the hospital. I replied that it was my opinion the hospital was dirty and I told him of my practice of trailing a finger along window ledges, the top of heart monitors and curtain rails in the wards and that trails of dust had come away, stuck to my finger. This practice of mine, started on the ships, became a repeated irritation for Paul for it embarrassed ward staff when I showed them what I had found. The paediatric ward sister burst into tears after one of my visits. The consultant paediatrician complained to Paul, who in turn complained about my behaviour. My response was that, instead of complaining, he should thank me for pointing out that the wards were not clean. I told him that an HCA would call in 'sick' and the ward sisters either would not report it or the domestic manager would, or could not, provide cover for absent staff. This business soured my early relationship with Paul but did result in the formation of an emergency crash team to clean any ward in difficulty. It was my old problem of getting senior nurses to become active ward managers. As usual, there were wards that were clean and others that were scruffy, mirroring the ward sister. I discussed my findings with my fellow Non Executives who gave me their support, and Chris Johnson of Bridgend, who had been Secretary of the Community Health Council, told me that he had been trying to get something done about the hospital cleanliness for some time.

During the debriefing after my first walkabout, I mentioned my anxieties about Glanrhyd, our mental health hospital, and was advised that discussions had started regarding refurbishment. I also commented upon my fears that some senior nurses were as institutionalised as the patients. When our new Nurse Director, Sue Gregory, arrived I told her about my anxieties which resulted in some early retirement and other changes in mental health care so that the most dependent of patients were cared for correctly and humanely.

My continued walkabouts were always followed by a meeting with Paul and he did not always welcome my comments. At the very least our early relationship was tricky. I had arranged for the four non-executive directors from Glan-y-Môr to accompany me on visits across the whole Trust. To my surprise, I discovered the non-execs from the old Bridgend Trust wanted to come on our visits to the Princess of Wales Hospital. They had not previously toured either the hospital or their other facilities. I learned that their Board meetings had rarely lasted more than 90 minutes where they were expected to be seen but not heard. It took several visits to cover the whole Trust area, but I believed that non-executives could not be expected to take decisions about institutions and services of which they had no visual or practical knowledge. I asked each non-executive director to accept responsibility for a group of clinical disciplines in which they would take a special interest and discuss any problems they found with me or the senior management. I was delighted by their response, but this action was not universally received sympathetically by the executive directors. Those from Glan-y-Môr were long used to the practice.

I chaired the monthly Board meetings on the basis that a non- executive director should not be expected to take a decision on a matter they did not understand. They had the right to question the executive directors if they wished and I expected them to make useful but short contributions to discussions. Of course, this doubled the length of the Board meetings which contained a standing item on the proposed new hospital. When discussing the 30 year payback term, I pointed out hospitals were designed to last only 60 years, at which the Chief Executive burst out, 'Oh Chairman, that is nonsense.' I said nothing but I was very angry and remained so throughout that day and night. The next morning I went to the Headquarters where I met Paul in his office. I told him I was the Chairman and he would never speak to me again in public in that manner. We then had a no-holds barred discussion. He told me I repeatedly interrupted his reading of reports, which I pointed out were included in the Board papers, with questions or comments. The Executive directors objected to being questioned by non-executives. I upset the ward staff, etc..

etc., - it all came out. I said the running of the Board was my job and as it was the non executives and not the executives who took the blame when 'shit hit the fan' not only had they to be fully informed, but they needed to know that standards were being maintained. I re-emphasised my primacy as Chairman and my long NHS record. We both agreed to compromises and essentially, from that meeting onwards, a working relationship developed between us which grew in strength and mutual respect and friendship. I remain convinced that the executives benefitted from the efforts of the non executives and that we assisted them to raise standards across the Trust. It certainly helped to have clean hospitals and low infection rates, which were to become national issues even though we had to find £250K to achieve this from our own resources.

The non-executives, who were drawn from a cross section of the population and political spectrum, all made significant individual contributions. David Cox was a retired army officer with a special interest in mental health; Mary Lee, a retired finance director from industry, maintained an interest in Trust finance. Chris Johnson was a retired Secretary of the local Community Health Council and previously a trade union official in Port Talbot Steelworks and had a special interest in the Princess of Wales Hospital. John Carr, my Vice Chairman, was excellent in dealing with the minutiae that I hated, e.g. standing orders. Charles Henrywood, a retired special needs teacher and previously Labour Council Leader for Neath, had a special interest in the needs of Neath and Port Talbot and virtually everything on the agenda. He was an inveterate, even irritating, questioner who added many minutes to Board meetings, but who often also uncovered potential problems. I protected his right to question more than once. David Davies was a retired social work executive and a trained mental and general nurse who was in close touch with the community of Neath Port Talbot and the needs of social and mental health. Professor Michael Harmer, from the College of Medicine, who had anaesthetised for me many times, and a very intelligent lady who was the Director of the National Lottery in Wales, Ceri Doyle. I met other UK Chairmen who said they never visited their patch other than on official occasions. How that worked I could not imagine. I asked for, and received, considerably more work from my non executive colleagues than was reasonable but, happily, they derived much satisfaction from being fully involved and they knew they made a pivotal contribution to the Trust's success. Senior NHS executives are often office or meeting-bound and cannot spend enough time in clinical areas. This is hardly surprising with the many demands of Government upon them but the result is a gulf between them and the clinicians which I hoped our non executives would bridge.

Paul Williams provided a strong leadership and gained the loyalty of his management colleagues with his forward thinking. I do not remember him ever congratulating me on anything I said or did and I do not believe he went out of his way to congratulate his colleagues. His habit was to say – now you've done that, why not do more or do it better? His leadership was also derived from loyalty to his staff and from his management skills and foresight and hard work. He attracted good staff. Politically he was astute, and correct; he never said in public what he might believe or regret unless his audience wanted to hear it. He knew everybody, was in all of the right organisations, including the Masons, and he established a rapport with his clinicians by providing them with excellent facilities in which to work, whilst still remaining in budget. His wife also worked in the NHS as a senior manager and as they were without children he devoted his energies to his work and river fishing. He was at his desk by 7.30 a.m. and often attended meetings late into the evening. He was a worker and an achiever. I decided I could best complement him by stressing the requirement of quality care, complimenting staff when justified and demanding improvement when required. I emphasised the need for staff to think of Bro Morgannwg and not Bridgend or Neath Port Talbot. I made the point of answering critical articles or letters in the local newspapers which misrepresented our intentions or actions. Paul and I established a good working relationship and I like to believe in due course he tolerated my walkabouts as their benefits became obvious.

Paul made great demands on his executive colleagues but, by attracting people of calibre, they achieved success. The Bro Morgannwg Trust became the standard setter in Wales. Two years after I retired from the Chair, a retired surgeon from Swansea, when admitting they had tried to scupper both the Glan-y-Môr Trust and the hospital and the Bro Morgannwg Trust, said that the combination of Paul and me had run rings around them. In 2009 Bro Morgannwg merged with the Swansea trust with a takeover of the management. What a turn around. I hoped the Swansea overspend could be corrected by the Abertawe Bro Morgannwg Trust without damage to the citizens of Bridgend, Neath and Port Talbot. This has not proved to be the case.

When I was first appointed to the Glan-y-Môr Trust in 1995, it had considerable autonomy which was gradually whittled away as day-to-day service decisions were made by Ministers and Welsh Assembly civil servants after the 1997 and 1999 elections. The most unreasonable of these was the annual bail-out of overspending Trusts. Cardiff, Swansea, Newport and several smaller Trusts repeatedly overspent by many millions. Each year Jane Hutt took the populist decision to fund their overspending. At least £123m was given to them over the years, whilst spurious recovery programmes were demanded but never completed. Unpopular management action and politically difficult decisions never happened and the overspending continued. The three or four Trusts out of 16 that managed their services and did not overspend were punished, along with the population they served, because they did not get any of the extra cash to compensate them. Our own clinicians demanded we overspend so as to catch up but we rejected doing so. I repeatedly reminded the Minister of this situation which I am sure contributed to her later decision to retire me.

My earlier anxieties about Bridgend personnel not having the determination to build the new hospital were unjustified. Indeed, a new momentum was imparted to the negotiations of the Final Business Case (FBC) by Paul Williams, the Director of Planning, Paul Stauber and the Directors of Finance, Edgeley Thomas, Eiffion Williams and his deputy, Huw Llewellyn, who had special skills. As the Treasury continued to rethink the rules and the final business case had not only to satisfy the financial needs of the Health Authority and the financial and political requirements of the Assembly, it was a jungle in which to negotiate. At the same time, two Trusts and their staff and clinical services had to be merged and managed. Planning a new hospital continued and, as we had deliberately maintained good working relationships with Baglan Moor Healthcare PLC, our clinical staff were fully involved and consulted by them.

The final business case was completed and the contract negotiations then proceeded. Finally, arrangements were made for us to go up to London to sign the contract in the consortium's solicitor's office. There the final drama of crossing the t's and dotting the i's and satisfying last minute legal niceties lasted all day and into the early hours. Paul and I started to sign contracts somewhere about 2.00am. The consortium raised £69m in the London market and building would take 30 months. We returned to Wales elated.

The good relationships we enjoyed with Baglan Moor Healthcare plc. and the constructors paid off handsomely. Clinical staff were repeatedly consulted during the building and fitting out of the hospital. Jane Hutt availed herself of the photo opportunities, and the staff of Neath General repeatedly visited the site to see its progress. This was important, for only essential maintenance was possible on the old building and it began to deteriorate.

When the buildings and their surrounds were finally completed ahead of schedule and in budget, we transferred all clinical services from Neath General, starting early one morning and admitting our first emergency patient that evening. It was a triumph for both the management and staff who worked extremely hard. On my previous walkabouts around Neath

General, I met several senior sisters who were alarmed at the prospect of working in the new building. Within a few days they had changed their minds. As we had maintained good relationships with the consortium, who in turn had consulted our clinical staff during their planning and subsequent phases, the hospital worked from day one. There were a few plumbing problems but nothing disastrous.

Another gratifying result of the new hospital was that the few Bridgend consultants who had been reluctant to work on two sites found the new facilities such a pleasure to work on that the rationalisation of our clinical services was soon complete. A major advantage in Neath was that the operating lists were not at the mercy of acute emergencies so that elective surgery could be planned with accuracy and firm appointments made. Before long our orthopaedic surgeons were making significant inroads into the waiting lists for joint replacement which was further assisted by a consultant who resigned from Swansea to work full-time in Neath. A feather in our cap.

It was agreed early on in the negotiations that the contract would include non payment if cleaning and maintenance fell below specifications, and we employed staff to monitor the service. The contractors had to employ more cleaners to meet the contract standards, but the cleanliness of Neath General was maintained in the new hospital and both sides were satisfied. There were national problems of medical staffing and we soon encountered problems in the minor casualty and obstetric units. We were unable to recruit specialist staff for the casualty unit and the paediatric cover for our obstetric unit which was provided from Dr. Dewi Evans' unit in Swansea was always the first to be withdrawn when Swansea was short. We had, by now, a computer system in radiology which allowed us to transmit images from minor casualty to the Princess of Wales Hospital. This enabled us to consider providing cover at night for the local accident centre by specially trained senior nurses. The Prince Philip Hospital at Llanelli, having the same problem, had closed their unit at night, bringing Jane Hutt's wrath upon them. The failure of paediatric cover for obstetrics also caused the frequent closure of our unit, often with women in labour, which was potentially dangerous. With the full support of the obstetricians in Swansea, we proposed to convert our obstetric unit to midwifery only, so that we could continue the delivery of the 60% of women who never needed a doctor for their ante-natal or labour care. This change of service required public consultation, led by the independent Community Health Council (CHC). Both our proposals for the casualty and midwifery unit were vehemently opposed by Noel Crowley, the Leader of the Neath Port Talbot Borough Council, and by local politicians, both elected and unelected. A petition asking the loaded question, 'Would you prefer a fully staffed, all purpose obstetric unit or a midwife led unit?' received about 10,000 supportive signatures. The local paper increased its sales supporting this objective. Of course, there never would be the staff or money available to provide full obstetrics and paediatric cover, but I believe you can get anyone to sign a petition presented in a shopping centre if you ask the right loaded question.

As the public consultation by the CHC proceeded, I repeatedly suggested that we meet the Neath Port Talbot Borough Council to explain to them what was intended, but without success. Councillor Dr. Dewi Evans, Plaid Cymru Councillor, had a letter published in the local paper which was a splendid example of 'shroud waving'. He listed every obstetric/paediatric complication he could find in the books and suggested the M4 to Bridgend or Swansea would soon be covered by women and the new born. I rebutted his letter, stating that we were acting on the best advice of our consultant obstetricians, whilst Dewi Evans had no special knowledge or expertise in this matter. The usual flow of ill-informed letters continued from militants but more worryingly for me were the repeated headlines in the newspaper quoting Noel Crowley, alleging that we were downgrading the hospital and depriving patients of proper care, etc., etc.

I am not sure now who called the meeting, but the Chairman and Chief Executive of Neath Port Talbot LHB and the Trust were asked to meet Noel Crowley. We arrived at the Civic Centre to find only the Council's Chief Executive, Ken Sawyer, present. I had long believed that he did not dare to contradict Crowley. Crowley arrived several minutes later and immediately, and aggressively, attacked Dr. Ed Roberts, the Chairman of the LHB, for the bad publicity appearing in the local press. Roberts, a very reasonable individual, explained quietly why and on what the LHB was consulting. Crowley paid not one iota of attention and repeatedly questioned why he had to keep reading about downgrading, bad publicity and why were we destroying goodwill, morale, etc., etc. I could feel my anger building through all this and when, for the umpteenth time, Crowley repeated 'then why do we have these terrible headlines in the paper?', I burst out, 'because they keep printing the rubbish that you keep repeating!' I let rip at him for some time and then there was absolute quiet. I could see shock on the faces of all those present. When Crowley next spoke his voice was quieter and more reasoned. My adrenaline was in full flow by now and I felt disappointed it was over. The meeting continued in a reasonable fashion. I should have lost my temper with him several years earlier.

With the public consultation complete, the CHC gave full support to our midwifery proposals. Protected by strict protocols, this unit and domiciliary delivery had become an essential part of managed child birth in the area and remains extremely successful and favoured, not only by our ladies, but also women living outside of the Trust area. The service provided by the LAC and its night-time nursing cover provides care for more patients than it did in its original form. By making these changes we were able to keep services going despite medical staffing shortages, which surely is an example of managing within resources. I remain unaware that any patient has suffered from our decisions and the M4 was not filled with ladies or babies in extremis. When the hospital was ready for its official opening, I learned Prince Charles was to open the new blast furnace at the nearby Port Talbot Steelworks. Enquiries were made through channels and it was agreed he would come to the hospital after the Steelworks. The opening went off remarkably well in the sunshine and the Prince of Wales was delightful. I trust the First Minister and the Health Minister enjoyed their visit and the day as much as our own patients and staff. The Neath Port Talbot Hospital was the only new general hospital in Wales since the Royal Glamorgan opened in 1999.

By the second year, the hospital won first place in the National PFI/PPP build awards, had achieved a Charter Mark and had won other awards at the end of the full year. I sought to have the Queen's agreement to have the Royal prefix added to the hospital's name and sent my request to the Welsh Assembly for support. Having had no reply and discovering my request had not been forwarded to London, I then wrote to the Secretary of Staff for Wales, Peter Hain, MP for Neath, but received a reply from Dough Toughey, his Minister, that my request was inappropriate. I believe the Royal Neath Port Talbot Hospital would have pleased everybody. The Royal Glamorgan had gained their honour before it was even opened. It is a strange world, but then a different political party was in power. I believe we would not have the Neath Port Talbot if Labour had been in power in 1995. Their ability to centrally finance hospital new build had been abysmal.

I had enjoyed the several variations of my career to varying degrees (dentistry, medicine, consultant practice, medical politics, hospital management and ten years of chairmanship). The latter ten were unplanned and unexpected and gave me great satisfaction. I would always criticise politicians of all parties if I thought what they were doing was not in the best interests of patient care and I pressed the case for the Glan-Y-Môr and Bro Morgannwg Trusts, with the Welsh Assembly Government. I gained the greatest satisfaction from the completion of the Neath Port Talbot Hospital. I am confident it would not have been built had I not been Chairman of Glan-y-Môr and Neath General had closed in 1997. The herculean efforts of the Trust management were crucial. The Bro

Morgannwg Trust was responsible for its completion and not the Chairman of Iechyd Morgannwg Health Authority or the then Leader of the Neath Port Talbot Borough Council, as both claimed when Hugh Thomas was made a Freeman of Neath and Port Talbot.

I had been pleasantly surprised to be appointed Chairman of Bro Morgannwg in 1999, when I was already 67 years old and a critic of the proposed Trust reconfiguration. I had been a repeated critic at meetings chaired by Jane Hutt. I was called to meet her, ostensibly to have an annual appraisal in the autumn of 2004. She told me that the Trust had achieved every target and set standards for others to follow. I had achieved everything expected of me. She believed that public servants should retire when they had reached their pinnacle rather than take too long to fade away. I nearly laughed aloud thinking 'unlike politicians!' She told me that in view of my age, I should give somebody else a chance to chair Bro Morgannwg. I was 72 and could not see the future NHS improving; I had by now had a hip and knee replacement and back problems so I did not object.

Several weeks later advertisements appeared seeking my replacement. To my surprise I was sent an application form. Paul Williams suggested I should fill it in as it might not be possible to find a suitable replacement and they would like to know I could continue until one was found. I therefore sent this form back, suitably filled in. A short list was drawn up but not before I received a telephone call from the Welsh Assembly's Director of Personnel requesting me to withdraw my application as the Minister wanted a clean sheet for the appointment committee to 'avoid complications'. As there was no point in carrying on in the face of ministerial opposition, I agreed. No appointment was made and I was requested to carry on, which I did for a further six months. Win Griffiths, Labour MP for Bridgend, then retired from Parliament. He received a phone call from the Assembly after which he applied for the post and was appointed Chairman of the Bro Morgannwg NHS Trust. So much for Nolan principles. I had completed 48 years of service in the NHS when I finally retired.

After I retired, aged 73, Brian Gibbons the then the Health Minister, wrote that I had 'been an outstanding Chairman' which was much appreciated. It remains a pleasure to view the Neath Port Talbot Hospital from the bypass as I drive to or from Pembrokeshire. Paul Williams became the Director of the NHS in the Assembly for which he worked even longer hours for a new Health Minister, Edwina Hart. They did away with the LHBs and brought back seven authorities very similar to the old Health Authorities. C'est la vie! When Paul retired from the Assembly Government he was knighted. Good managers in the NHS were scarce.

25 Conclusion

After the health minister ended my career as a chairman my memoir should have ended though I continued to provide reports on Grievous Bodily Harm cases for the Crown Prosecution Service or the defence, and occasionally attended court. In essence I am now retired and enjoy life, despite increasing disability due to osteo-arthritis.

My career in some respects started when as a schoolboy I decided upon Medicine. My failure of the Higher School Certificate was life and character changing and I don't believe my self-confidence totally returned.

Even after I was proceeding up the ladder I was aware I was walking on thin ice, particularly when in conflict with people in power. The decision to do so was influenced by my parents and their belief, often stated, that 'If a job is worth doing it is worth doing properly'. Although I do not believe in God I retained vestiges of my mother's Christianity.

Honesty and integrity guided me and the need to complete any task I had accepted to the best of my ability. This resulted in my saying what I believed rather than what was politic or what others wanted to hear. I have my supporters and several critics.

I have, however, had a satisfying and reasonably successful career with several diversions making a contribution to the final product. I look back upon a mixture of regrets, mistakes, and yet several successes. I wish both of my parents had been able to share these with me.

26 An Unwelcome Finale

Before I was retired at 75 I had had a replacement right hip and knee. My lower spine became more troublesome and was affecting my walking. I was able to play and walk nine holes of golf using a walking stick (but not on the greens!). Gradually, my right hip caused me increasing difficulty and pain. I was 79 when I consulted the surgeon who had operated when I was 64. The femoral component of my metal hip had loosened and all required replacement.

I attended the pre-op anaesthetic assessment clinic and gave the nurse the history of my heart, carotid arteries, collapsed lumbar spine and drugs. I was admitted on a March afternoon by the orthopaedic associate specialist but the anaesthetist did not come to discuss how he proposed to anaesthetise me. Next morning I met both consultant surgeon and anaesthetist in the anaesthetic room of the operating theatre. A spinal injection with epidural pain relief and sedation was offered and accepted by me.

What followed was reported in the British Medical Journal January 12th 2013. (See appendix: 'How no one acted when they should have'.

After I got home and learned the new tricks of personal plumbing I wrote to the President of the Royal College of Surgeons of England. I explained my predicament and highlighted my belief that the failure of the orthopaedic staff to visit me post-operatively had turned a medical accident into a personal disaster. I questioned who was in charge of my care if the orthopaedic team did not visit me.

I received a reply full of sympathy but no comment on the absent ward visits. I wrote again with the same result.

Meantime I had paid for, and received, a copy of my in-patient's notes. There was a paucity of written reports from nurses and doctors. The junior doctor who catheterised me on the first post-operative morning had not recorded this in the notes. There were no fluid balance charts. I wrote to the Chief Executive of the Health Board with a list of complaints. Much later I received a reply which included a 'profuse apology for a failure of a duty of care'. A root cause analysis of my complaints and treatment by a team of clinicians and managers had recommended this.

Interestingly it was pointed out that I had been restarted on Clopidogrel (an anti-platelet drug which prevents blood clots) on the first post-operative morning whilst I had an epidural catheter in place. This conflicted with all guidelines. I did not think this made a significant difference for I had woken up with my numbness. The orthopaedic associate specialist must have come in early to do this and check the motor power of my legs. I do not believe he would not have noticed the urine bag on its stand had he come after I was catheterised. In my sedated state I believed my numbness was the result of the epidural as I had been advised by the nurses.

However, urinary retention, and the gas and mucous escaping from between my legs raises the possibility of a spinal lesion in my mind. I dragged up 'cauda equina syndrome' from my memory but associated it with trauma and protrusive spinal disks. I had no knowledge that they too were rare complications of spinal and epidural injections.

It became increasingly clear that my signs and symptoms were not going to clear and also that no communication was taking place between nurses and doctors. On the Sunday I told my wife of my anxieties and she spoke to a house surgeon who had not previously spoken to me. 'Yes' she said 'they knew I had a problem which would be dealt with the next day.' Later that evening my daughter was able to galvanise the consultant into calling the junior staff. Interestingly he denied all knowledge of my complications and said that 'surely you don't expect me to see your father at this time'-it was about 9.30 p.m. on Sunday. He visited me on Monday morning and I do not remember him doing this again.

When I left hospital after a seventeen day stay I knew that my injury should have been investigated and surgically decompressed within 8 to 12 hours. I decided to raise the problem of the failure of surgeons to review their patients in the immediate post-operative days and to sue the University Health Board. Only by creating a fuss would I make those in authority think about current clinical practice. I did not want a confidentiality clause to stop me.

As I had had no satisfactory reply from the President I submitted a motion to the Annual General meeting of the Royal College Surgeons on June 21st 2012 which Bill Heald, an international colo-rectal surgeon, past Vice President of the College and a good friend, seconded.

'That this meeting requests the Council of the college to consider:-

That the breakdown of the surgical team concept and the failure of some consultants and their staff to carry out ward rounds raises the question of who is in charge of the inpatient's care?'

I had two minutes to present my case in which I described what happened to me and why. Bill was overseas and the President cut short the discussion by saying everybody supported the use of ward rounds. The motion was passed with applause and one against. I was surprised that Council did not discuss the motion until October and disturbed that nothing has since emerged from the Council, Editor or President of the

Royal College of Surgeons.

Therefore I wrote 'A patient's Journey' article published in the BMJ on January 12th 2013. My solicitor advised me against this, saying 'Don't upset the other side'. I replied that I didn't care about the other side, only patients. I did not wish to be closed down by confidentiality clauses. The other side had accepted full liability and causation anyway. My 'journey' attracted some interest and correspondence.

In March 2013 I was asked to take part in a conference organised by the Faculty of Dental Surgery of the Royal College on the future of the NHS. I was reluctant to do so because I could only think about the present NHS. 'OK then, give us twenty minutes on your views of the present NHS.' After, the Dean asked me to publish my presentation in the Faculty Journal-reproduced here.

The government used to meet the medical profession at the Joint Consultants Committee (JCC). This was formed from the Conference of Royal Medical Colleges and the BMA. The College Presidents and Deans considered themselves superior to the BMA representatives because their target was improving patient care and not salaries and working practices. The BMA thought the Colleges politically naive allowing the Governments to succeed in gradually imposing management control of the professions. We wondered if the carrot of a knighthood, which most Presidents gained, was the price paid. One RCS President, Terence English, later Sir Terence, virtually told the Chief Medical Officer that you don't need to be medically qualified to do surgery, when with the support of his council, he asked that his nurses be allowed to take out the saphenous veins used in coronary artery replacement. In the preliminary JCC meeting I spoke against this proposal saying that varicose veins and hernias would follow. 'No' said the President, 'we will monitor the situation.' Now we have numerous non-medical staff doing intermediate surgery whilst the junior medical staff are seriously underexposed to surgical training.

What started as a simple memoir intended for my children has now grown into a small book. This is due to Andrew Sadler, a retired maxillofacial surgeon, and now a researcher, reading a few pages. I am so grateful for his contribution and that his hobby has caused me to widen my horizons. I regret I cannot finish my memoir on a happy note but of one thing I am certain. Through my life and career I have benefitted from medical care from involved, capable and ethical medical professionals. That I have reached 81 is proof of their skills and professional care. Long may this continue after I am history.

Since the above was written I have been readmitted for the second time with clot induced urinary retention. I have been bleeding from a small vessel for a period of time which reduced my haemoglobin to 7 gms % half the normal reading. I had four units of blood transfused – a first for me.

I have had over fourteen episodes of haematuria with two emergency admissions. Experts advise that I will not improve further, my hip operation has a very long tail which grew from the agreement made by the Government in 2003 to pay a huge pay increase for consultants whilst limiting their recognised paid work to 40 hours a week. For some, if ward visits were not timetabled they were not done. The politicians have attacked the very ethics of our profession.

The End

Appendix 1 How No One Acted When They Should Have

Russell Hopkins and Gavin Werrett

First published in the British Medical Journal 12th January 2013 Reproduced with permission.

In June 2011, aged 79, I was admitted to the orthopaedic ward of my local NHS teaching hospital for a revision of a loose 14 year old hip replacement. I was clerked in by an orthopaedic associate specialist but no anaesthetist arrived.

Next morning I met the consultant anaesthetist and the surgeon in the anaesthetic room. I recognised the anaesthetist as having given me a spinal block for a previous knee replacement. He proposed a combined spinal and epidural block with heavy sedation, to which I agreed.

I was returned to the ward about 4 pm. The orthopaedic associate came to tell me that all had gone as planned, and he confirmed my ability to raise and extend my legs. When the nurse started my routine checks I told her that I was completely numb in and around my groin. Later my wife was present when I again told nurses of my numbness. We were reassured by their explanation that the area was the last to recover and this might be delayed by the epidural pain relief. Even then I remembered I had not experienced this when I had my knee done.

When it was time to sleep I advised the nurse that I had not passed urine but had no desire to do so. As I was on intra-venous fluids, I was surprised when I woke the next morning at about 6 am that I didn't need a bottle. However, I could palpate a supra-pubic swelling, which I assumed was my bladder, even though pressure on it was not uncomfortable.

I asked for a doctor as I believed I needed catheterisation. About 8 am a junior doctor arrived. After palpating my abdomen he called for a catheter tray and relieved me of about 1.5 litres of urine, although I was unaware of any manipulation.

Leaving me with an indwelling catheter attached to a bed bag, he departed without, it turned out, making any record in the notes or reporting to a senior doctor.

As it was a Friday, I expected a visit from the orthopaedic team, but only a specialist nurse in pain relief came to see me. I had minimal discomfort. In the afternoon I found I was lying on a wet sheet, with copious mucus covering my buttocks. As the nurses changed the sheet they discovered that the epidural tube had come out of my back which must have contributed to the wetness. That evening in my wife's presence I told the nurses my numbness was unchanged despite the loss of the epidural at an unknown time. One nurse suggested I would soon recover if she got into bed with me. I was amused, my wife was not.

On Friday night I could not sleep and requested night sedation, for which the duty doctor was called. When he arrived, after considerable delay, he was the same doctor who had passed my catheter. I learnt that he was the general surgical foundation year 2 doctor covering orthopaedics out of hours. On Saturday morning, my only visitor was a specialist nurse from orthopaedics, who said he would ring the anaesthetist, and the pain relief nurse. Subsequently I learned the anaesthetist was on annual leave and unavailable. By now I was aware of the uncomfortable numbness involving my buttocks and posterior thighs. Gas bubbles escaped in the mucus between my legs.

Sunday continued in a similar vein; I was confined to bed by foot pumps and without any medical visit. When my wife arrived in the late afternoon I told her of my increasing concern at being unable to raise medical interest in my condition, the aetiology of which had to be more complicated than delayed epidural recovery. My wife spoke to a houseman, who told her my problems would be dealt with on Monday. When my wife returned home, she rang our daughter, a consultant rhinologist who rang the ward and was told that the registrar could not be called because I was not an emergency. My daughter fortunately was able to ring the orthopaedic consultant at home to ask him, 'What is wrong with my father?' About 9 pm, three junior doctors came in turn, armed with pins to contemplate the possibility of a cauda equina syndrome. On Monday morning I had a visit from the orthopaedic consultant, who ordered that I be starved in case of the need for further surgery. I then had an emergency magnetic resonance scan, and in the early evening the report was reviewed by a spinal surgeon, who told me of a haematoma lying posteriorly at L1-L2 and that he considered surgical decompression was not justified. The window of opportunity to bring a possible early recovery thus remained closed.

Space limitation does not allow the description of the unpleasantness of the two and a half weeks I spent in hospital. Care of incontinence was not on the same level as the kindness of the nurses. The urinary bed bag was changed to a flip-flow valve and, after discharge, to intermittent catheterisation. Both were easy to forget in the absence of bladder sensation, which led to several 'accidents' when abdominal pressure was raised—for example, when standing or coughing.

After discharge, four episodes of haematuria, one of which caused an emergency admission, resulted in prolonged antibiotics and an attempt by my excellent urologist to get me off Clopidogrel. Eight months after the operation I have stopped using catheters. My bladder started to function weakly at about seven weeks after surgery and gradually improved. It remains weak and lacks sensation. When I stand, a pain-like sensation tells me I must urinate. Fifteen minutes later I can pass almost the same amount again.

The back end remains a problem. I am not incontinent but I have some problems differentiating between gas and solids. The district incontinence service introduced me to the self administered Peristeen rectal washout system, paid for, as were the urinary catheters, by my general practice's budget.

Now that the rectal catheter has been redesigned and the balloon does not burst, this is an excellent system, which prevents 'accidents'. However, the process is time consuming and there is a learning curve. I cannot empty normally but require the combination of abdominal muscle contraction, manual compression, and agitation of the abdomen. I use the Peristeen system almost every day.

The profound saddle anaesthesia has made a partial recovery. The perineal and buttock areas are dulled and paraesthesic. The perianal tissues have sensation but this is abnormal and the area feels isolated from the surrounding tissue. There is no sensation produced by the passage of solids.

Initially I seemed to be sitting on a log that was very uncomfortable. Now the sensation is of sitting on a leather strap with my tuberosities unprotected. The literature states the elderly male has a poorer prognosis for a full recovery with this presentation. Time will tell. Happily my hip functions reasonably well and I am due to have a knee replacement in about a month's time.

NHS healthcare delivery is rarely out of the media and there are frequent reports of misadventure.[1] Medical students are apparently trained in teamwork and communication but not in the care of the ill. The presidents of the Royal College of Physicians and the Royal College of Surgeons have warned of the effect on junior doctors of the European Working Time Directive, shift work, days off, reduced hours, and clinical experience. Doctors' numbers may have increased but not their expertise. Similar problems exist in the nursing profession as nurses train to do the work that was previously the remit of doctors while leaving nursing to healthcare assistants.

The secretary of state for health has recognised there are problems in the NHS at weekends owing to the absence of senior doctors. My recent difficulties result from all of the above. Additionally there is a failure to train doctors and nurses adequately. If the discipline of anaesthesia recognises that central nerve blocks can cause complications with serious implications for patients, all of the staff who provide postoperative care must be trained to recognise them.[2] Reluctance to contact senior staff for advice must be eliminated.

Note taking and communication between nurses, between nurses and junior doctors, and between junior and senior doctors require rethinking. If consultants stop doing ward rounds and supervising junior doctors, it is necessary to redefine who is ultimately responsible for patient care. Instead of spending vast sums settling negligence claims (£1bn in 2010), would this money not be better used to provide increased staffing and training, particularly for out of hours care? As a non-medical friend said to me, 'If they can't even look after you, who will they look after?'

1 Royal College of Surgeons of England. Emergency surgery, standards for unscheduled surgical care. RCSEng, 2011. www.rcseng.ac.uk/publications/docs/emergency-surgery-standards-for-unscheduled-care/

2 Cook TM, Counsell D, Wildsmith JA. Maior complications of central neuraxial block; report on the third National Audit Project of the Royal College of Anaesthetists. Br j Anaesth 2009:102:179-90.

Appendix 2 A Memorable Patient in the Bad Old Days

Originally published in British Medical Journal. 9th April 2005. Reproduced with permission.

I embarked on medical training in 1961 as a mature student with two years of general dental practice and three years of hospital oral surgery and Maxillofacial trauma behind me. My second six month preregistration post was as a surgical house officer at a busy London hospital. My responsibilities spread over four firms, each headed by a teaching hospital consultant and included 60 beds on-take alternate weeks with an additional 60 to cover, plus casualty at night time. The experience of 'hands on' general surgery, urology, and gynaecology was fantastic, but so was the fatigue.

One evening I was called to casualty to find a hugely obese, partially collapsed lady, bleeding copiously from the vagina who had missed a couple of periods. Her pulse was weak, her blood pressure barely recordable, and her major veins impalpable. As I started to catheterise the patient to provide fluid, I sent for the resident surgical officer (who was 10 minutes away at a dinner), O+ blood, and the theatre team. I was told that the team was already working at a nearby hospital. By the time the surgical officer arrived, resplendent in his dinner jacket, fluid was running in nearly as fast as the patient was losing blood.

He made a rapid decision to operate. 'No theatre team or anaesthetist available', I told him. After a few seconds he said, 'Hoppy, you give the anaesthetic.' I had had considerable experience of dental anaesthesia and had given gaseous anaesthetics to patients in casualty for minor surgery, so with the confidence of youth and ignorance I agreed.

The porter had not yet returned with the blood, so the two of us pushed the patient's trolley to the lift, with me keeping fingers on her carotid pulse. It became impalpable, and I said, 'It's too late; she's gone.'

The top half of the patient raised up and said, 'No I've not gone yet.' After that embarrassment, we got her to theatre and somehow, using wooden poles, lifted her on to the theatre table.

The surgeon took off his dinner jacket and brought in the theatre packs of instruments. Not having the confidence to use thiopentone (pentathol) or knowledge of the patient's weight, I opened up the gas, oxygen, and trichloroethylene of the Boyle's machine, applied the facemask, and pushed the patient's mandible forward in the approved manner. By the time the surgeon was ready, her eyelash reflexes had gone, and she seemed relaxed. He opened the abdomen, sucked out pints of blood, and somehow identified and clipped off the ectopic pregnancy. We felt elated: job done, crisis over.

A few seconds later, however, and the patient was attempting to get off the table. Clearly her relaxation had owed more to hypovolaemia than anaesthesia. The surgeon held on to her from inside the abdomen, and I held down her shoulders while I opened up the trichloroethylene. This pantomime gradually subsided, and the surgeon was able to finish his work and close up the wound. By this time the porter had arrived with the blood, which we pumped in.

The next morning we found our patient sitting up eating a hearty breakfast without any memory of the previous evenings surgery. So ended my anaesthetic career. It is worth adding that the patient's wounds healed without infection.

The memory of these events, which some readers may find difficult to believe, has never left us. Today such a patient would not be admitted to a hospital so ill prepared to deal with a life threatening emergency.

Nowadays, I expect there would have been a major investigation as a result of a critical incident report and even possible disciplinary action. (The management refused to reimburse my colleague for the dry cleaning of his blood stained trousers.) On the other hand, a life was saved by the courage and initiative of the resident surgical officer, whose surgical training had included considerable operative practice.

Appendix 3 A Personal View of Today's NHS

Originally published by the The Royal College of Surgeons of England. Fac Den J 2013. Reproduced with permission.

I was reluctant to accept the invitation of the Vice-Dean to participate in a meeting called to discuss a modern, future National Health Service (NHS). I told him I was an angry old man, 80 years old, more concerned about today's NHS than the future. I was angry because much of the spirit that built and maintained the NHS, in which I had spent 48 years, had been dissipated by politicians, civil servants and managers, and the contracts they had negotiated.

I haven't just become angry. I have been angry for years and a nuisance to politicians of both main parties. The late Norman Whitehouse, a past secretary of the British Dental Association, told me I wasn't a politician. I thought this was a compliment.

In 1980 The Daily Telegraph reported me telling the British Medical Association (BMA) conference that the BMA could not always seek more government money for the NHS without a stop to the wastage of money it already had. I referred to over-prescribing, over-investigating, over-treating, failing to do clinics and operating lists, and keeping patients in hospital for non-clinical reasons.

In the early 1980s I attacked the policy of the BMA leadership: 'You, the management, give us the money; we, the doctors, will heal the sick — and n'er the twain shall meet.' My experience of being chairman of the medical staff of South Glamorgan and on the area team of the health authority had convinced me that management of the NHS would always fail unless clinicians were actively involved. I still believe this to be true.

In the mid-1980s The Sunday Times reported me telling the BMA conference that some senior NHS staff were more comfortable than their patients and that we had to consider the interest of patients instead of just our own. I referred to those staff who ran their service to please themselves without thought of the consequences of their behaviour (e.g. doing the operations they enjoyed while leaving varicose veins and hernias to rot on the waiting list).

I therefore welcomed the Griffiths NHS management inquiry in 1983.[1] Through my membership of the Central Committee for Hospital Medical Services (CCHMS) and its subcommittees, I persuaded my colleagues to ask Griffiths to include clinicians among those considered suitable to manage the service. On the advice of American consultants, the previous

Labour government had introduced line management in which the major staff groups managed themselves in parallel lines without any cross-over control. For example, nursing lost control of cleaning and there was nobody in overall charge of a hospital or a health authority. The chairmanship rotated on the area team. Making decisions was a time consuming and frustrating exercise.

I welcomed the introduction of general management and agreed initially with the Thatcher government as it started to reduce the power of consultants. Many of them had abused their power and influence while those in London persuaded Thatcher that all NHS consultants used NHS time and salaries to do private practice. However, the last 30 years has seen managerial reduction of consultant power morph into attacks on elitism, professionalism, ethical practice and the pursuit of excellence. In the healing professions, the concept of quality patient care based on long-established ethical professional practice has been a casualty.

The combination of politicians, civil servants, target and tick box driven centralised management, plus educationalists, trade unions, the BMA and Junior Doctors Committee, the Royal College of Nursing, Modernising Medical Careers and the European Working Time Regulations (EWTR) is now producing a continuous torrent of bad news from across the UK, headed by the Mid Staffordshire disaster. Recently, I watched a series of documentaries from the impressive neurosurgery unit in the John Radcliffe Hospital only to read of a survey claiming 38% of NHS staff would be reluctant for their relatives to be admitted in their own hospitals.[2][3]

The paradox, sadly, is that when politicians finally find the courage to implement necessary changes to the delivery of healthcare, the local population, fuelled by opportunists in politics and the media, invariably demands no change.

Research from the University of Edinburgh published in the BMJ has shown that the medical graduates are confident about teamwork and communication but know little about the diagnosis and care of the ill patient.[4] In many medical schools, the exposure of undergraduates to ward work, clinicians, consultants and the sick is minimal. I listened recently to a Today programme interview where the Royal College of Nursing secretary claimed that the nursing degree included a 'lot of ward work'. I have spent time as a patient and watched the trainees following their mentors around the wards looking and listening but not doing anything. No wonder compassion and care of the elderly is poor; I have read of graduate nurses who 'don't do sick'.[5]

Healthcare assistants who are untrained and might not be capable of being trained above a minimum level are left to do many tasks considered previously to be nursing. The nurses meanwhile perform many of the tasks that were once those of junior doctors and, sadly, we have lost the dependable state enrolled nurse in the quest for 'status'.

You may have read of the nurse who retired in 2012 after 55 years of service. She said that when she qualified at Guy's Hospital she could run a ward. Now graduate nurses must start from scratch. Imagine learning to drive only by watching the driver. When the old type of nurse retires, they take compassion and patient care with them.

The net result is that universities produce doctors and nurses that are not fit for purpose. I do not know about modern dentistry but retired colleagues tell me that dental graduates are not dissimilar.

In medicine, the repair of this problem is endangered by the EWTR. Shift work ensures the loss of the continuity of care. An inpatient may not see the same doctor twice and the consultant junior team responsible for a patient is no more. The consultant name on the bed or wall is meaningless. The danger of the loss of the continuity of care is that the subtle signs of a patient deteriorating can be missed. If consultants and responsible juniors fail to do ward rounds, nobody is in charge of the patients' care. An inquest in Colchester disclosed that a very ill patient was only seen and examined by an F1 trainee with four months of experience.[6] The coroner's reports might be summarised as reflecting a situation where nobody was in charge.

I have had a consultant tell me he doesn't do ward rounds because his junior staff are no longer there and anyway why should he work out of hours when general practitioners don't? We must have the return of the consultant-junior doctor team, and clinical responsibility for postoperative and routine care. 'Some senior NHS staff are more comfortable than their patients' is as true today as it was in the 1980s.

If you want a laugh and to read about the 'bad old days', look up the BMJ issue in which I reported a most memorable patient.[7] In 1964 a morbidly obese West Indian female patient was bleeding to death from haemorrhage from an ectopic pregnancy. Her life was saved by a resident surgical officer (RSO) who, in his dinner suit and trousers, opened the abdomen while I gave my last anaesthetic. There were no other theatre staff available. The last sentence of the article reads: 'a life was saved by the courage and initiative of the RSO, whose surgical training had included considerable operative practice'. The BMJ cut the rest, in which I commented on the paucity of the experience of modern surgical trainees and wondered whether future consultants would be competent to look after us in our old age.

Compare this story with an anecdote from a urological friend who was recently taking a trainee though a nephrectomy: 'Take care around the back — there are lots of little bleeders there and we don't want to be back here tonight looking for one.' 'I won't be here', replied the trainee. 'I'm off shift.' Would you trust this trainee with your relatives?

In 2012 the BMJ published my own patient's journey. I described my hip replacement of June 2011, in which I sustained a spinal column bleed from the spinal/epidural central nerve block. This gave me the full triad of a cauda equina syndrome. The bleed was a medical accident but the failure of postoperative care was gross negligence. Everything I have described previously conspired to prevent a diagnosis being made in time to prevent permanent damage. I was looked after by healthcare assistants and, when seen by junior doctors or nurses, despite drawing attention to my belief that something was wrong, nobody recognised my symptoms for what they were or raised any concern. No orthopod visited.

The system failed me at all levels and we should not forget the politicians, civil servants and managers who made it all possible. I recall an issue of the BMJ that carried a story of a retired general practitioner whose father, a retired anaesthetist aged 90, was admitted for a repeatedly postponed endoscopy. He died of dehydration and renal failure. How could this happen? The last sentence of my journey in the BMJ reads: 'As a non-medical friend said to me 'If they can't look after you, who will they look after?'[8] Unless things change, everybody should wonder that.

Negligence now costs the NHS over £1 billion per annum.[9] Should those responsible face the prospect of a disciplinary procedure? Settling negligence cases takes so long that nobody is held responsible and I remain deeply cynical about claims that 'lessons have been learned'. Because of staff changes, these lessons must be re-learned and re-taught repeatedly. Six months after my hip replacement I was readmitted - to the same hospital - for a knee replacement. While there, I asked the nurses and healthcare assistants whether they had received instructions on cauda equina syndrome and the complications of central nerve blocks. Nobody knew what I was talking about, despite this being a recommendation of the investigation into my complaint. Where are the lessons that have (supposedly) been learnt?

The Telegraph published a letter from Professor Charles Galasko, a past chairman of the hospital recognition committee of the RCS.[10] He claimed, probably correctly, that the Mid Staffordshire scandal would not have occurred if the College still had this role. I claim also that had I been the chief executive or chairman of the managing authority, the Mid Staffordshire fiasco would not have happened.

In 1985 I was appointed general manager of the University Hospital of Wales, the University Dental Hospital and Ely Hospital - the largest unit in Wales and among the largest in the UK. I had no training in management and must have been a risk. How did I change a dirty, overspent and underperforming hospital into a clean, efficient, in-budget hospital, refurbished in the wards and high tech areas?

I headed a team of six senior managers and relied on common sense derived from a clinical background plus a knowledge of whole body healthcare. As a surgeon, I was used to taking decisions and sticking to them. Furthermore, as a past chairman of medical staff and a member of the health authority area team, I knew how bad some managers were. I was well aware that some consultants were just as bad in their own way and could not be allowed to continue their bad habits. Finally, I was the son of my father, a self-made manager and leader who took me with him when I was a child to the tram and bus depots for which he was responsible. He spoke to all staff and heard about problems first hand.

As general manager, I made repeated, unannounced visits to all parts of my three hospitals. When I found a problem, I called the person responsible. I forbade my management team to be office bound. We were one team without boundaries, and our eyes and ears were always open. The managers had to be visible and communicate with the staff. I have searched for a long time for a word that describes the reluctance of NHS managers to leave their offices to visit clinical areas. I believe some are embarrassed they might do something wrong and certainly some clinicians are arrogantly rude to them in clinical areas. However, many clinicians never see or meet senior management and there is little two-way communication. This is a fundamental problem.

I chaired two NHS trusts for ten years after I retired at 63. When I was 73, the health secretary asked me to step down to give 'somebody else a chance'. That person was a retiring member of Parliament, who, by coincidence, was in the same party as the health secretary.

'Blue-rinsed' ladies or elderly businessmen usually have one thing in common with retired trade union officials or party members: little knowledge of healthcare delivery. They therefore consider themselves inferior to their executive colleagues and cannot call them to account. Too often chairmen and non-executives appear to be appointed as a reward for political services and rarely do more than attend board meetings or appointment committees, on which they can be an embarrassment. As a chairman, I continued my 'walkabouts' but I requested my non-executive directors take special interest in the clinical disciplines of their choice. They too made regular visits, talking to staff and patients. Each month we all met to discuss our findings and recommendations. I then met with the Chief Executive.

I also encouraged my non-executives to question the executive at board meetings and told them never to vote on anything they did not understand. Initially, one chief executive took umbrage at my actions but recognised their value when independent reports on our hospital were praiseworthy.

The Mid Staffordshire debacle was a failure at board as well as at management and clinical levels. The Francis report recommends[11] that Board level staff should have a common code of ethics, standards and conduct and that Directors of NHS bodies should have a 'fit and proper persons test'; those who fail should be removed and disqualified from similar posts.

No specific recommendations were made about the non-executives. They must be able to hold the board executives to account. To do this, they must know about healthcare delivery, and they must have the time and commitment to visit their hospitals regularly. The government must rethink the role of the non-executive director. Retired clinicians with an understanding of the function of the board could assist in this.

The involvement of clinicians in management must continue but their professional ethic must be reinforced rather than compromised. Safe, quality, patient care must be their target. If we wish doctors and nurses to diagnose and treat the sick competently, then the government must consider the clinical content of undergraduate courses. The EWTR must not be allowed to destroy continuity of patient care. The consultant firm and responsibility for the patient must be restored.

References

1. Department of Health and Social Security. NHS Management Inquiry (1983) Report (The Griffiths Report). London: HMSO; 1984. Available here: http://www.sochealth.c0.uk/national-health-service/griffiths-report-october-1983/ (cited 31 May 2013)

2. NHS staff survey: 40% would not recommend health service to family. The Guardian. 20 March 2013. http://www.guardian.co.uk/society/ 2012/ mar/20/ nhsstaffssurvey-health-service (cited 31 May2013).

3. NHS Staff Survey - 2012 Results. National NHS Staff Survey Coordination Centre. http://www.nhsstaflfsurveys.com/cms/ (cited 31 May 2013).

4. Victoria R Tallentire VR, Smith SE, Wylde K, Cameron HS. Are medical

graduates ready to face the challenges of Foundation training? Postgrad MedJ 2011; 87: 590-595.

5. Ann Clwyd to head review of way NHS handles complaints. BBC News. 15 March 2013. http: // www.bbc.co.uk/ news / health-21785732 (cited 31 May 2013).

6. Pensioner's hospital death 'due to confusion caused by NHS targets.' The Telegraph. 21 February 2013. http://www.telegraph.co.uk/health/9886053/ Pensioner hospital-death-due-to-confusion-caused by-NHS-targets.html (cited 31 May 2013).

7. Hopkins R. In the bad old days. BMJ 2005;330:824. Available here: http:// www.bmj.com/content/330/7495/824 (cited 31 May 2013).

8. Hopkins R, Werrett G. How no one acted when they should have. BMJ 2012; 345: e5366. Available here: http://www.bmj.com/content/345/bmj.e5366 (cited 31 May 2013).

9. Scrap rules banning NHS care in negligence pay out cases, says doctors' defence body. The Telegraph. 11 January 2013. http://www.telegraph.co.uk/ health/healthnews/9795398/Scrap-rules-banning-NHScare-in-negligence-payout-cases-saysdoctors-defence»body.html (cited 31 May 2013).

10. The Government must have known about the damaging culture in the National Health Service. The Telegraph. 18 February 2013. http:// www.telegraph.co.uk/comment/letters/9876166/The-Government must-have-known-about-the-damagingculture-in-the-National»Health-Service.html (cited 31 May 2013).

11. Francis R. Independent Inquiry into Care Provided by the Mid Staffordshire NHS Foundation Trust, January 2005-March 2009. London: TSO; 2010.

Appendix 4 Daily Telegraph Article

Published December 14th 2013. Front page article.

CONSULTANTS yesterday called for proper staffing of NHS wards at weekends after a retired senior surgeon was left disabled following poor care from junior doctors.

The surgeons spoke out in a letter to The Daily Telegraph, saying that patients were being put at risk because inexperienced hospital staff were being forced to take on too much responsibility.

The countries most senior doctor is preparing to publish recommendations to put the NHS on a seven day footing. There has been increasing concern about worse care and far higher death rates for patients treated towards the end of the week. Next week Prof Sir Bruce Keogh, the NHS medical director, will demand changes to increase the number of senior doctors working weekends, after research found that 4,400 patients die each year because staff cover is inadequate.

Russell Hopkins, a retired surgeon, and former Wales BMA chairman, was left with nerve and bladder damage after hip surgery in June 2011.

The operation was on a Thursday. He was left for days without seeing a consultant as his condition worsened. Despite his pleas and those from his daughter, he was not seen by specialists until Monday, four days later.

He was found to have complications that caused permanent damage to his bladder and nerves.

Earlier this year, a study of four million patients found that those who had surgery on a Friday were 44 per cent more likely to die than those who had the same operation on a Monday. The risks steadily increased as the week went on.

Mr Hopkins, 81, is among six retired surgeons and two serving consultants appealing for reforms to hospitals.

They said the introduction of the European working time directive, limiting surgeons' hours, had destroyed a system under which senior doctors took responsibility for all patients in their care.

Next week, Sir Bruce will call for changes in the way hospitals are run, to improve care at weekends. But Mr Hopkins said he was concerned that proposals already produced did not go far enough to improve patient safety.

He said: 'My anxiety is that some of the proposals just aren't good enough. If you have just had hip surgery it's no good seeing an eye doctor.'

The eight consultants say failings by the NHS had repaid Mr Hopkins's lifetime of service with negligence and long term disability.

In the letter, published today, they say many surgeons 'yearn to put ethics before directives' and take responsibility for the patient on whom they operated.

The letter calls for a return to the system that predated the working time directive, with doctors organised into firms each with a named head 'with whom the buck stops'. It says: 'No working time directive can absolve surgeons of their responsibility to the patient on whom they have operated.'

***

<u>Surgical teamwork</u> A letter originating and coordinated by RH.

SIR — Before retiring, the final signatory of this letter was a surgeon and general manager of a large university hospital. The after-care of a hip operation failed him catastrophically, the NHS repaying a lifetime of service with negligence and long-term disability.

We, the other signatories, are experienced consultants who share his analysis of how the system failed him and why it fails so many others.

Any surgeon who performs an operation needs to be part of a team that shares an understanding of the possible complications. Surgery is too large and technical for a shift system of junior staff.

Similarly, a consultant gastro-intestinal surgeon is not competent to tackle an orthopaedic emergency. There is no effective substitute for the team or firm system, with a named head with whom the buck stops. No 'working time directive' can absolve surgeons of their responsibility to the patient on whom they have operated, and this can only be shouldered if shared with their trainees.

Many surgeons yearn to put ethics before directives and to practise these old-fashioned, fundamental values. Sadly, the NHS has taken away their teams and split up partnerships. Now a good measure of the quality of a surgical unit is to observe senior surgeons on the wards at weekends.

Shift work must be replaced by surgical firms Patients need to know the name and face of the consultant responsible for their care, so they can learn how the operation went, its outcome, what follows and when they can go home.

   Julian Elkington, FRCS
   Prof RJ Heald FRCS
   John S Kirkham FRCS
   Prof Khursheed Moos FRCS
   Anthony B Richards FRCS
   Robert Walters FRCS
   Michael H Young, FRCS
   Russell Hopkins, MRCS, FDSRCS
   Cardiff

Printed in Great Britain
by Amazon.co.uk, Ltd.,
Marston Gate.